TOOLS FOR
WORKPLACE
SUCCESS

Essential Skills for the Workplace

Mc Graw Hill Education

Bothell, WA • Chicago, IL • Columbus, OH • New York, NY

www.mheonline.com

 **Education**

Send all inquiries to:
Contemporary/McGraw-Hill
130 E. Randolph St., Suite 400
Chicago, IL 60601

ISBN: 978-0-07-661063-1
MHID: 0-07-661063-2

Printed in the United States of America.

4 5 6 7 8 9 RHR 15 14 13

The **McGraw·Hill** Companies

Contents ...

Introduction ...

Today's employers want employees who have all the skills they need to be successful in the workplace. Having—and being able to apply—academic skills such as reading and mathematics remains important. However, the jobs of the 21ˢᵗ Century require employees to have skills that go beyond these core academic competencies. Employees must also be able to manage themselves, make thoughtful decisions, communicate effectively in writing, and use 21ˢᵗ Century tools to solve problems.

The *Workplace Skills: Essential Skills for the Workplace* series helps you develop competencies that are highly valued in today's knowledge-based economy. Each scenario-based lesson within *Tools for Workplace Success*, *Writing for Work*, and *Applied Computer Basics* focuses on the skills most often identified by employers as keys to career readiness. Lessons also provide opportunities to discuss and apply these skills.

Workplace Skills: Tools for Workplace Success

In the workplace, personal and interpersonal skills are as important as technical and academic skills. For example, employers expect their employees to be organized, self-controlled, and able to listen to others. Traits and skills such as these will better prepare you to get a job, keep it, and advance in your career. Each of the four themes in this book focuses on a set of desirable traits and skills. The lessons within these themes will help you learn how to apply these traits and skills on the job.

Theme 1: Meeting Workplace Expectations focuses on traits and work habits desired by all employers, such as being reliable and dependable.

Theme 2: Working with Others focuses on interacting effectively with people from diverse backgrounds and building good working relationships.

Theme 3: Managing Yourself focuses on self-control and self-management skills, such as being responsible and professional.

Theme 4: Getting Ahead focuses on skills and behaviors that are important for advancing in a job or career.

Remember!

Interpersonal skills, such as effective speaking and listening, will be important during the interview and later on the job. Speaking effectively can be important when promoting an idea, requesting time off, or furthering your own job goals. Listening effectively can be critical when following up on an oral assignment or when collaborating with a coworker.

Tools for Workplace Success

Making the Most of Each Lesson ■ ■ ■ ■

Each lesson focuses on a group of desirable skills and behaviors. Lesson examples are based on realistic workplace scenarios. All lessons are divided into three sections—Skill Examples, Try It Out!, and On Your Own. Each lesson models a set of skills and behaviors, provides practice in analyzing employees' actions, and provides opportunities for you to respond to scenarios on your own.

Skill Examples To start each lesson, you will read two scenario-based workplace examples and analyze the actions of the employees and the consequences of those actions. By comparing these examples, you will be able to identify the positive and negative aspects of each scenario.

Try It Out! In this section of the lesson, you will learn how employees respond to and solve workplace problems. You will also have the chance to consider how each employee solved the problem and what the consequences were.

Regardless of the problem, it is important to consider relevant information and alternative solutions before choosing a solution. You can use the *Decision-Making Process* chart to help you make a decision:

Decision-Making Process				
STEP 1: Identify the Problem	**STEP 2:** Locate, Gather, and Organize Relevant Information	**STEP 3:** Generate Alternatives	**STEP 4:** Choose a Solution	**STEP 5:** Implement the Solution
What is the problem that needs to be solved?	What information is available to me?	What are some possible solutions to this problem?	Which solution should I choose?	What can I do to implement the solution?
What decision needs to be made?	Which pieces of information are relevant to this problem?	What are the potential consequences of these solutions?	Why is this solution better than the alternatives?	Whom do I need to communicate with about my solution?

On Your Own This section of the lesson provides several opportunities for you to apply what you have learned to realistic workplace scenarios.

Within each lesson, *Remember!* notes highlight essential life and career skills.

Remember!

Every employee needs some basic skills to succeed in the workplace. These skills include:

- **Communication Skills:** Employees should be able to speak effectively, listen actively, and observe their surroundings for information.
- **Interpersonal Skills:** Employees should be able to cooperate with others, resolve conflict, and negotiate.
- **Decision-Making Skills:** Employees should be able to identify problems, consider relevant information, and choose a solution.
- **Lifelong Learning Skills:** Employees should not stop learning once they are in the workplace. They should take responsibility for improving their skills.

Meeting Workplace Expectations ...

Most employers expect their employees to behave in a professional manner and to possess certain traits and work habits. While expectations may vary from one workplace to another, some are common to all employers.

In Theme 1, you will learn about standard workplace expectations.

Lesson 1: Dependability and Reliability Dependable and reliable employees can be counted on to complete their tasks correctly and within a reasonable time frame. *Objectives include*:

- Being Punctual
- Complying with Policies
- Fulfilling Obligations
- Attending to Details

Lesson 2: Getting Organized Being organized helps employees easily locate information and successfully complete important tasks. *Objectives include*:

- Managing Stressful Situations
- Monitoring Details
- Reporting Progress and Status of Tasks
- Organizing Your Work Area

Lesson 3: Verifying Information Employees who make sure that information is complete and accurate help the company operate efficiently and make effective plans. *Objectives include*:

- Maintaining Logs
- Detecting Errors
- Obtaining Information
- Completing Forms

Lesson 4: Customer Satisfaction Employees who provide a high level of customer service create loyal, satisfied customers. *Objectives include*:

- Understanding Customer Needs
- Providing Personalized Service
- Acting Professionally
- Keeping Customers Informed

Key Factors for Meeting Workplace Expectations ▪ ▪ ▪

These lessons are intended to help you identify and practice behaviors necessary for meeting workplace expectations. Employers expect employees to consistently demonstrate basic work habits. These habits are the building blocks on which employees improve, advance, and ultimately show their worth. To effectively and consistently meet workplace expectations, you must be able to:

- **Be organized** Organization improves employees' efficiency and effectiveness while also keeping stress to a manageable level.

- **Practice self-management** Working independently shows employers that not only can you meet expectations but that you can do so with minimal management or supervision.

- **Cooperate with others** Cooperation is necessary for customer satisfaction. Employers expect employees to understand customers and meet their needs.

Knowing how to meet workplace expectations will make you more valued as an employee.

Lesson 1
Dependability and Reliability

Regardless of your career or position, being dependable and reliable is essential. Employees with these traits show their supervisors that they are responsible, care about their work, and can be counted on. Dependable and reliable employees fulfill their obligations on time, carefully and effectively complete their tasks, and follow all regulations and policies that are in place.

Skill Examples

Being Punctual After submitting their résumés to several companies where they are interested in working, Brandon and Justine have both been asked to come in for an interview.

Read the two examples and answer the questions that follow.

EXAMPLE 1 Brandon's Interview

> Brandon has a job interview for a bank teller position tomorrow morning at an unfamiliar location. He was instructed to arrive at 8:00 A.M. and to ask for Allison Griffin. He was also told that he would be required to take a brief math test. Brandon spent the night before his interview practicing for his math test, making sure his suit was ready to wear, and planning his route to the bank. Before going to bed, he double-checked his alarm clock to make sure it was set correctly for 6:00 A.M. Brandon arrived for the interview on time.

1. How might Brandon's actions influence Allison Griffin's opinion of him?
   A. She might think that Brandon has strong math skills.
   B. She might think that Brandon is unreliable and cannot be counted on.
   C. She might think that Brandon follows instructions and fulfills obligations.
   D. She might think that Brandon is not motivated to work at the bank.
   E. She might think that Brandon does not dress professionally.

2. What would probably have happened if Brandon had not spent the night getting ready for his interview?
   F. He would have performed well on the math test.
   G. He would have had to meet with Allison Griffin on a different day.
   H. He would have showed he was dependable and reliable.
   J. He would have been unprepared and late for his interview.
   K. He would have had to meet with a different bank employee.

EXAMPLE 2 Justine's Interview

Justine has a job interview tomorrow morning with a local community college for a clerical position. She was told to arrive for the interview at 9:00 A.M. with three copies of her résumé and a list of references. She was also told that she would be expected to take a computer skills test. Justine stayed up late to prepare for the interview and prepare a list of references. The next morning she selected her clothes and planned her route to the interview. Justine then remembered that she needed to print the extra copies of her résumé. By the time she printed the copies she was late leaving and missed her train. She arrived for the interview at 9:30 A.M.

3. What impression might the interviewer have of Justine based on her behavior?

    A. She would be a reliable and dependable employee.

    B. She communicates effectively.

    C. She does not follow instructions and is unreliable.

    D. She has excellent computer skills.

    E. She is very motivated to work at the college.

4. What would probably have happened if Justine had been better prepared the morning of her interview?

    F. She would have performed better on her computer skills test.

    G. She would have been on time for the interview.

    H. She would have selected a more professional outfit.

    J. She would have been able to reschedule the interview.

    K. She would have been able to walk to the interview.

Think About It Think about Brandon's and Justine's actions. What impression do you think each made on the interviewer? Which one of them is more likely to be hired? In forming your answer, think about the following questions:

- **Preparation** How did Brandon and Justine prepare for their interviews, and how did it affect them the morning of their interviews?

- **Responsibility** In what ways did both Brandon and Justine demonstrate responsibility to their interviewers?

Remember!

Self-Management
Sometimes it is not possible to meet every deadline or fulfill all your obligations. Both work-related and personal obstacles occur all the time. When you realize that you are unable to fulfill an obligation, it is important to clearly communicate this to the appropriate people. In *Example 2,* Justine misses her train and knows she will be late. By calling her interview contact to say she will be late and by working to find a solution to the problem, Justine can show that she is dependable and reliable.

Try It Out! ■ ■ ■

Complying with Policies Carlos was recently hired as a cashier at Dean's Delicatessen. On Sunday afternoon, he received the following voice mail from his manager providing him with instructions for his first day of work.

> *Hi Carlos, this is Kyle from Dean's Delicatessen. I wanted to let you know that work starts at 9:00 A.M. on Monday. Please arrive a few minutes early, so you can clock in on time and the manager on duty can show you around before you get started. Our standard uniform is a white button-down shirt and black pants. You'll also need to wear slip resistant dress shoes. If you have any questions you can call me at 555-0112. Thanks, Carlos. We'll see you on Monday.*

Carlos does not have the correct shoes, and he does not have time to buy a new pair before work the next day. Carlos has a pair of slip resistant sneakers that he thinks should be fine, but he does not want to get in trouble on his first day. He is unsure about what he should do.

Remember!

Take Responsibility for Learning Your first day on the job is your chance to make a good first impression. Make sure you understand and follow all company policies and procedures. If you are unclear about a policy or do not know what the company's policy for a particular issue is, it is your responsibility to ask your supervisor or manager. Carlos checks with his manager to confirm the dress code and determine if the shoes he has are acceptable or if he will need to buy new shoes.

Decision-Making Process				
STEP 1: Identify the Problem	**STEP 2:** Locate, Gather, and Organize Relevant Information	**STEP 3:** Generate Alternatives	**STEP 4:** Choose a Solution	**STEP 5:** Implement the Solution
Carlos does not have the correct shoes to wear to work.	Carlos does not have time to buy new shoes before work on Monday. Carlos has sneakers that are slip resistant, but he is supposed to wear dress shoes.	Carlos can wear the sneakers since they are slip resistant. Carlos can call Kyle to explain his situation and ask if the sneakers are okay to wear.	Carlos does not want to ignore the dress code, but he does not want to be late to work either. He chooses to call his manager to check if his sneakers will be okay.	Carlos calls Kyle and explains his situation.

Carlos has a pair of slip resistant shoes that he thinks will be acceptable, but he does not want to ignore the dress code on his first day. Carlos's first option is to buy new shoes, but since he does not have time to do so before work, he needs another alternative. Unsure about what to do, Carlos calls his manager to explain his situation and see if they can arrive at a temporary solution. The manager understands Carlos's situation and allows him to wear his sneakers on Monday. He also tells Carlos that he will need to have the proper attire by the start of the workday on Tuesday.

Fulfilling Obligations Janie works as a receptionist at a law firm. She often has to work on many important tasks at the same time. On Wednesday morning she receives the following e-mail from one of the firm's partners.

E-mail Message

To: McClelland_Janie@DCH.org

Subject: New Contact Lists for Clients

Janie,

As you know we've recently made several new hires, and juggled some of our resources to handle our increased case load. Our contact lists will need to be updated to reflect these changes. Please complete the lists and send the updated version to each of our clients by the end of the day.

Thanks, Janie.

Linda Dewey

Janie spends most of her morning working on routine tasks, such as answering the phone and greeting guests. After lunch, she confirms catering deliveries for several meetings the following week. Then another attorney asks her to copy files for a trial he has on Friday. After she finishes copying the files, she begins working on updating the contact lists but is unable to complete the task before the end of the day.

1. Which of the following is a potential consequence of Janie's not completing the contact lists?
   A. Clients may not be able to get in touch with their lawyers.
   B. The food may not be delivered to the meeting on time.
   C. Lawyers at the firm will not be able to contact each other.
   D. The attorneys will not have the correct files that they need.
   E. Clients may not receive their bills.

2. What should Janie have done differently to make sure she completed her task?
   F. She should have told Linda Dewey she could not do that task today.
   G. She should not have answered phone calls.
   H. She should have e-mailed clients the old contact lists.
   J. She should have made the contact lists her first priority.
   K. She should have asked someone else to do the job for her.

Reflect In both of the *Try It Out!* examples, the employees had to decide what course of action to take. Do you think they made the correct decisions? What were the positive and negative effects of their actions? What other actions might they have taken? How might the outcomes of the situations have changed based on a different set of actions?

Remember!

Cooperate with Others Part of being dependable and reliable is understanding the role you play as a part of the larger company. The work you do impacts others. If your work is not done well, or on time, it may impact the success of another individual or the company as a whole. Just as you may need to depend on others to help you succeed in your work, others may depend on you to successfully complete your tasks. Janie's inability to prioritize an important task and complete it on time may negatively impact the firm.

On Your Own ▪ ▪ ▪

Read the following scenarios. Then answer the questions that follow each scenario.

SCENARIO A Being Punctual

You are a gardener for a local landscaping company. You take the bus to headquarters every morning where you clock in and are assigned to a team. Then you take a company truck to the job site.

> Monday is a holiday and your bus will be running on an alternate schedule. Fewer buses will be running, which means that the time in between runs will be longer. You have the option of taking a bus that will arrive either 25 minutes earlier or later than your regular bus.

Complete the chart below and then answer the questions that follow.

Decision-Making Process				
STEP 1: Identify the Problem	**STEP 2:** Locate, Gather, and Organize Relevant Information	**STEP 3:** Generate Alternatives	**STEP 4:** Choose a Solution	**STEP 5:** Implement the Solution
The regular bus service has been changed. You need to find a different way to get to work to ensure that you arrive on time.	Your regular bus is running on an alternate schedule. You can leave 25 minutes earlier or later than usual.			

1. What solution did you choose to implement for this problem?

2. Who, if anyone, needs to know what you have decided? How would you communicate this to that person?

SCENARIO B Complying with Policies

You are an early childhood education specialist at a local day care. The day care has a policy that requires employees and children to stay home if they have a fever and to not return until they have been fever free for 24 hours.

> You wake up on Wednesday morning and feel achy and tired. You check your temperature and find that you have a fever of 100.5°. You have unpaid sick leave and do not want to miss two days of work and pay.

3. What problem do you need to solve?

4. What are some possible solutions to this problem? What are their consequences?

5. Which solution would you choose to implement?

SCENARIO C Fulfilling Obligations

You work as a chef in a hotel. You occasionally work overtime for special events.

You have been scheduled to work at a wedding this Saturday night. You have tickets to a sporting event that night and try to find someone to cover your shift for you, but none of the other chefs is available that evening. You know from previous events that there is usually more than enough staff on hand for these types of special events, and you do not want to miss the game.

6. What are some alternative solutions that you could take to resolve this situation?

7. What are the positive and negative consequences of the solutions you listed?

8. Which solutions would show that you are dependable and reliable?

SCENARIO D Attending to Details

In your work as an administrative assistant, you are often asked to write brief notices.

Your supervisor has just reviewed a recent notice you wrote informing the office about a change in the vacation policy. She has given you a hard copy of the document with her changes marked on it. She asks you to make the changes in the electronic file and then send out the notice to the entire office. It is after 5:00 P.M. when you finish, and you are anxious to leave, but you are not sure that you entered all of the corrections accurately.

9. What alternative actions might you take and what might their consequences be?

10. Which alternative would you choose to implement?

11. Based on your solution, do you think your employer would view you as a reliable and dependable employee? Why or why not?

Summary ▪ ▪ ▪

Employees who are dependable and reliable are trustworthy and complete their tasks. To ensure that you are dependable and reliable, be sure to do the following:

- **Fulfill your obligations** Follow through on commitments and meet deadlines.

- **Be punctual** Show up for work and appointments on time.

- **Pay attention to details** Always check your work to make sure that it is free of errors and that all details have been considered.

- **Comply with policies** Follow all company directions, policies, and procedures.

Answers begin on page 122.

Lesson 2 ■ ■ ■
Getting Organized

Planning and organizing do not come naturally to everyone, but they are essential skills that you should have. In the workplace, being organized can help you carry out important tasks. It can make it easy for you to monitor details or provide progress reports. By planning and preparing for your tasks, you will be able to do your job better.

Skill Examples ■ ■ ■

Managing Stressful Situations Lakesha and Jeremy both have challenging schedules. They often work on multiple projects during the same day or week.

Read the two examples and answer the questions that follow.

EXAMPLE 1 Lakesha's Weekly Routine

Lakesha works as a school guidance counselor. Three days a week, she has morning meetings with students. On each of these days, she might have meetings with several students scheduled back-to-back.

> Lakesha does not have time between meetings to review each student's file. She needs to find a different solution. At the beginning of each week, Lakesha collects files for all the students she will meet with that week. Then, she sets aside time in the morning on each counseling day to review the files. She takes careful notes on the topics she plans to address with the student. She also places flags and sticky notes on relevant pages in each student's file. This helps her be prepared in case she needs to reference the information during the counseling session.

1. How does Lakesha's organization benefit her?
    A. It gives Lakesha a single solution to all of her students' problems.
    B. It makes Lakesha the fastest guidance counselor in the school.
    C. It allows Lakesha to cancel unnecessary meetings.
    D. It makes it possible for Lakesha to take on more students.
    E. It helps relieve stress because Lakesha is prepared.

2. If Lakesha did not review each student's file before the meetings, what would probably go wrong during the counseling session?
    F. Lakesha would not have enough information about that student to offer effective guidance.
    G. Lakesha would lose interest in helping her students.
    H. Lakesha would make up new issues to discuss with the student.
    J. The student would congratulate Lakesha on her lack of preparation for the counseling session.
    K. The student would be late to the counseling session with Lakesha.

Remember!

Self-Management

When your workload feels challenging, take a step back and think about the ways you can get organized. For example, you can create to-do lists or color-code files. Being organized will help you prioritize tasks and make sure that each part of a task is completed thoroughly. In *Example 1*, Lakesha sets aside time to organize her day. She takes notes and places sticky notes in the files to identify issues she wants to discuss with each student. As a result, Lakesha is prepared for her busy day ahead of time and feels less stressed.

Tools for Workplace Success

EXAMPLE 2 Jeremy's Weekly Routine

Jeremy works as a house painter for a large residential developer. He is often assigned to two or three job sites each week.

> Jeremy must work on multiple job sites. He purchases materials for each site all at once to save time during his busy workweek. However, Jeremy is not in the habit of making lists or being organized. Sometimes, when he is placing orders for paint and supplies at the beginning of a week, he overlooks the needs of one of the job sites. Last week, Jeremy purchased the wrong types of paint. He ended up with too much indoor white paint. He also forgot to buy the outdoor beige paint he needed to complete his work on one of the sites.

3. What might the consequences of Jeremy's actions be for his employer?

   A. His employer might need to hire additional house painters.

   B. His employer might need to give Jeremy a bonus to cover the cost of the extra white paint.

   C. His employer might need to ask Jeremy to use white indoor paint on the outside of a home.

   D. His employer might lose money on unneeded supplies and could fall behind schedule on the project.

   E. His employer might need to sell the house without having it painted.

4. What would probably have happened if Jeremy had written a list of required materials for each job site?

   F. He would have wasted time by having to return to the paint store to buy the correct paint.

   G. He would have given his employer a good reason to hire an additional house painter.

   H. He would have purchased the right amounts of each type of paint he needed.

   J. He would have found some old outdoor paint and used that at the job site.

   K. He would have asked his employer to ship the correct paint to the site.

Think About It Both Lakesha and Jeremy had busy workloads that caused them stress. Which of them effectively used organization to prepare for their week and better handle the stress? In forming your answer, think about the following questions:

- **Self-Management** What solutions did Lakesha and Jeremy develop to help manage the stress of their busy schedules?

- **Organization** Who was able to find the materials needed to perform his or her tasks?

Remember!

Allocate Resources

Organize and inventory your tools and materials before you begin a project. Create a checklist of all the items you will need for a job. Refer to the checklist to be sure you have everything you need before you begin. If you find that you are missing materials, you have the time to gather what you need or identify an alternate plan for completing the project. This will help save time later on, because you will not have to stop and look for missing materials. In *Example 2*, if Jeremy had checked his materials and made a list of the supplies he needed, he would not have wasted time and money going back to the paint store.

Try It Out! ■ ■ ■

Monitoring Details Mollie is an acoustics technician at a symphony hall. She is currently working to set up the hall for a visiting orchestra.

As the week comes to a close, Mollie realizes that she has not set up an important piece of equipment. She reads through her log of materials that have been shipped to the hall. This piece of equipment is not on the list. Mollie needs to set up this piece of equipment before the visiting orchestra's first performance. The performance is in just a few days.

Mollie's employer must have forgotten to include the piece of equipment on the request list. The only way to get this piece of equipment is to have it shipped. However, Mollie is worried that standard shipping may be too slow.

Decision-Making Process				
STEP 1: Identify the Problem	**STEP 2:** Locate, Gather, and Organize Relevant Information	**STEP 3:** Generate Alternatives	**STEP 4:** Choose a Solution	**STEP 5:** Implement the Solution
Mollie does not have a critical piece of equipment she needs to prepare the symphony hall.	The equipment was not ordered ahead of time. The only way to get the equipment is to have it shipped. The equipment may not arrive on time if it is shipped via standard delivery.	Mollie can ship the equipment via standard delivery and hope it arrives on time. Mollie can have the equipment shipped via overnight delivery.	She chooses to notify her supervisor of the situation and requests that the equipment be sent via overnight delivery.	Mollie places the shipment order, and the equipment arrives the next day.

Mollie does not realize she is missing an important piece of equipment until she is almost finished setting up for the concert. Mollie's first option is to ship the missing item using a standard delivery method. This is what she typically does. However, she is not sure that the item will arrive in time for the concert. She decides that the item will need to be shipped using overnight delivery. This is more expensive, but Mollie knows she will get the equipment before the concert. She explains the situation to her supervisor and receives permission to have the equipment shipped overnight. Mollie is relieved that she followed up about the missing item, though a little late. She learns that it is important to make sure ahead of time that all the required pieces of equipment have been ordered and that they have arrived well before she starts her work.

Remember!

Monitor and Correct Performance Plan to periodically review your performance. This will help ensure that your tasks are performed correctly. If you make an error, you should recognize it, fix the problem, learn from your mistake, and improve your performance. You should also work to improve areas where you are not as strong as you should be. When Mollie recognizes that the equipment is missing, she finds a solution to make sure her work is done well and on time.

Reporting Progress and Status of Tasks Harold works as a truck driver for a courier company. He makes many local deliveries during the course of the day. Harold is scheduled to make a particular delivery by the end of the business day on Tuesday.

Unfortunately, Harold underestimated the amount of time some of his earlier deliveries would take. By Tuesday afternoon, Harold knows he will not be able to make his final delivery before the end of the day. Harold does not mind making the delivery later in the day. However, he is worried that no one will be at the business to sign for the packages. Harold decides to wait until the next day to make the delivery.

1. How might the customer react to Harold's decision to wait until the next day to deliver the package?

    A. The customer will praise Harold for his decision not to disturb her after business hours.

    B. The customer will be upset that her package was not delivered on time.

    C. The customer will give Harold a tip when he arrives with the package the next morning.

    D. The customer will call Harold's supervisor to suggest Harold get a raise.

    E. The customer will give Harold a cell phone so he can inform her if her packages will be delivered late in the future.

2. What might have happened if Harold had called the customer on Tuesday afternoon to inform her of his scheduling problem?

    F. Harold would have prevented the customer from becoming upset at his late delivery.

    G. Harold would have tried to get to the business before closing time.

    H. Harold would have changed his schedule to deliver the package on time.

    J. Harold would have convinced the customer to accept the delivery from another driver.

    K. Harold would have learned if someone could sign for the package after hours.

Reflect In the *Try It Out!* examples, Mollie and Harold each needed to decide how to solve a problem caused by poor preparation. While Mollie chose to have a missing piece of equipment sent by overnight delivery, Harold decided to wait until the next day to deliver a package. Mollie's decision, though a little expensive, helped her complete her job on time. Harold's decision, on the other hand, resulted in a late delivery. What other solutions could Mollie and Harold have come up with?

Remember!

Decision Making

Sometimes you are not able to complete a task the way you would like to. You may run out of time or not have the resources needed to complete your duties. When situations like this arise, think about what the next best possible outcome might be. Then try to make that outcome happen. For example, Harold was unable to make his delivery on time. The next best outcome would have been to reschedule the delivery for a time that satisfies the customer.

On Your Own ▪ ▪ ▪

Read the following scenarios. Then answer the questions that follow each scenario.

Managing Stressful Situations
You are the lead carpenter for a home remodeling company.

> Your team is assigned a number of tasks to complete before the end of the day. Since all of your team members are busy on other projects, you begin working on these tasks yourself. While some tasks can only be completed by you, others can be completed by any team member. After three hours, you manage to complete less than half of the tasks. You will not be able to complete everything by yourself.

Complete the chart below and then answer the questions that follow.

Decision-Making Process				
STEP 1: Identify the Problem	**STEP 2:** Locate, Gather, and Organize Relevant Information	**STEP 3:** Generate Alternatives	**STEP 4:** Choose a Solution	**STEP 5:** Implement the Solution
You cannot complete your team's tasks by yourself in one day.	Some tasks must be done by you. Some tasks can be done by any team member.			

1. What solutions can you come up with that will allow you to complete all the tasks on your list without cutting any corners?

2. For the solutions listed, to whom would you need to communicate your solution?

SCENARIO B **Monitoring Details**
You work as a manager at a local poultry farm. One of your main responsibilities is to manage phone calls from corporate customers.

> One of your first phone calls of the day is from the manager of a restaurant that specializes in serving locally grown food. The manager tells you that he just received his delivery of fresh poultry, but he did not receive everything he had ordered. You review the order and immediately see a problem. The worker who placed the order did not fill out the order form completely. Some details were overlooked; this is why the restaurant's order was filled incorrectly.

3. Once you recognize the error in the order form, what problem must you solve?

4. What are some possible solutions to this problem?

5. What are the consequences of those solutions?

SCENARIO C Reporting Progress and Status of Tasks

In your job as a clerk at a local supermarket, you are responsible for taking weekly inventory of the frozen food section.

> Your manager asks for an update on the inventory log for the frozen food section. In response, you say that it is "going okay." You notice that your manager seems unhappy with your response, and you are unsure why.

6. Why is your response to your manager insufficient? What might your manager think of your answer?

7. How could your response to your manager have been more appropriate?

SCENARIO D Organizing Your Work Area

As part of your job as a receptionist for a graphic design company, you receive dozens of e-mails each day from clients and coworkers.

> One day, your supervisor reprimands you for not adhering to a new dress code that went into effect this week. You tell him that you had no idea about the code. He explains that all employees received an e-mail regarding the new code. He allows you to complete your day in your current outfit. When you get to your desk, you search through your e-mails. Because your e-mails are stored in one general in-box, it takes a long time to find the message.

8. What problem do you need to solve?

9. What are some possible solutions to this problem? Which would you choose?

10. What impact will your solution have on your daily work?

Summary ■ ■ ■

When your workspace is organized, you will be able to easily locate tools and information to get your job done. To get organized, be sure to do the following:

- **Organize your work area** Before you begin a task, make a list of everything you will need. Then make sure you have access to all of these materials.

- **Monitor details** During your workday, write important details in a notebook.

- **Report your progress and the status of tasks** Give your supervisors accurate and adequate information. This will help them make educated decisions toward meeting project goals.

- **Manage stressful situations** Developing strategies to stay organized and keeping your workplace neat will help you get through these situations.

Answers begin on page 123.

Lesson 3 ▪ ▪ ▪
Verifying Information

In the workplace, verifying information can help you and your company achieve goals. With accurate information, you and your company can make better plans and operate more efficiently. Verifying information includes completing forms, keeping logs, finding errors, and getting necessary information.

Skill Examples ▪ ▪ ▪

Maintaining Logs Ronald and Mary work at the same hospital as part of the janitorial staff.

Read the two examples and answer the questions that follow.

EXAMPLE 1 Mary's Cleaning Log

Mary works the night shift on the janitorial staff. She is responsible for cleaning all of the restrooms on the north side of the hospital. Mary always cleans her assigned restrooms but sometimes forgets to complete the cleaning log.

RESTROOM CLEANING LOG: NIGHT				
Location	6:00 p.m.	9:00 p.m.	Cleaned By	Date
Floor 1 North	√	√	Mary	3/17
Floor 1 South	√	√	Mark	3/17
Floor 2 North				
Floor 2 South	√	√	Mark	3/17

1. When Mary's supervisor reviews the log, what might he think?
   A. Nobody has cleaned the restrooms on the south side of the hospital.
   B. Mary did not clean the restrooms on Floor 2 North.
   C. Mary cleaned the restrooms later than she should have.
   D. Mary completed all her tasks on time.
   E. Mary received help from Mark in cleaning the restrooms.

2. What would Mary's supervisor think if Mary had filled out each section of the cleaning log?
   F. He would think that Mark had cleaned the north side.
   G. He would be assured that Mary had completed her tasks on time.
   H. He would be pleased that Mary had cleaned all of the hospital restrooms.
   J. He would be able to fire the rest of the janitorial cleaning crew.
   K. He would be concerned that Mary was doing too good of a job.

Remember!

Take Responsibility
When you think you are finished with a task, make sure you review your work. Check to make sure you have not made any errors. You should also check to make sure you finished the task completely. In *Example 1*, Mary cleans her assigned areas but does not complete the log, which is also part of her task.

EXAMPLE 2 Ronald's Cleaning Log

Ronald works the day shift on the janitorial staff. One of Ronald's job duties is to clean the patient rooms. He must do this after one patient has been discharged and before the next is admitted.

Ronald's job has to do with keeping the hospital environment sterile. He must be diligent when completing each of his cleaning tasks. Ronald recognizes that doing a thorough job will help prevent hospital-acquired infections from spreading from patient to patient. As soon as Ronald completes a task, he is required to update the room-cleaning log. His supervisor regularly checks the log to make sure that a particular room has been cleaned and that the log is being updated. Before Ronald declares a room finished, he reviews each note in the log. Doing so allows him to be sure he has not missed any areas that need cleaning.

3. What is the importance of Ronald filling out the log and verifying the information he puts in it?
   A. It shows that Ronald dislikes the work he does.
   B. It shows that Ronald knows how to fill out a log.
   C. It keeps Ronald's supervisor informed of the work he has completed.
   D. It proves that Ronald's supervisor does not trust him.
   E. It allows Ronald to lie to his supervisor about the work he has done.

4. What might happen if Ronald filled out his log incorrectly?
   F. Ronald might take a longer amount of time to clean rooms.
   G. Ronald might have to undergo training on how to fill out a log.
   H. Patients would always have clean rooms available.
   J. Some patients might be assigned rooms that have not been cleaned.
   K. Patients might be asked to clean their own rooms.

Think About It Mary and Ronald were both responsible for working independently. Their supervisors relied on them to update the logs to be sure they had completed their tasks. Which employee is more likely to be trusted with tasks that require greater independence? In forming your answer, think about the following questions:

- **Self-Management** How did Ronald and Mary show their supervisors that they could be trusted to be prompt in their work?

- **Communication** How might an employee's communication skills affect the supervisor's opinion of the employee?

Remember!

Understand Systems
Maintaining a log is important because it keeps track of what tasks have and have not been completed. In *Example 2*, Ronald carefully updates the room-cleaning log. This helps the other janitorial staff learn what tasks have been done. If Ronald does not update the logs, the hospital will be unsure which rooms are clean and dirty and might clean a room twice, causing a delay in a patient's room assignment.

Try It Out! ■ ■ ■

Detecting Errors Joellen is an assistant interior designer at a design firm. She is often responsible for discussing initial design plans with new clients.

> Joellen is working with a client to remodel a bedroom. During a meeting with the client, Joellen takes notes about what the client wants for her new bedroom and also takes measurements of the room. When Joellen reviews her notes later, she thinks she made a mistake when writing down the information. Her notes say that the bedroom has three same-sizcd windows. However, Joellen is certain she remembers seeing one large window and two same-sized windows in the client's bedroom.

Joellen knows that the senior designer will use her notes to develop a detailed sketch for the client. She does not want to waste the designer's time by providing him with the wrong measurements for the windows. It is extremely important that Joellen give the designer accurate information. This will help the designer create a sketch that best matches the client's needs. It will also help the designer provide the client with an estimate of how much the remodeling will cost.

Decision-Making Process				
STEP 1: Identify the Problem	**STEP 2:** Locate, Gather, and Organize Relevant Information	**STEP 3:** Generate Alternatives	**STEP 4:** Choose a Solution	**STEP 5:** Implement the Solution
When Joellen reviews her notes after a client meeting, she thinks she made an error.	The senior designer will use Joellen's notes to develop a detailed sketch for the client. Joellen is responsible for providing the senior designer with accurate information.	Joellen can use the information from her notes. Joellen can schedule another visit to remeasure the windows before presenting her notes to the designer.	She chooses to schedule another visit to remeasure the windows before speaking with the senior designer.	Joellen remeasures the windows in the bedroom, and then presents her revised notes to the senior designer.

Joellen must submit the correct window measurements to the senior designer. However, she is not sure if her notes are correct. Her first option is to trust her notes and submit them to the designer. However, submitting incorrect information could lead to an incorrect cost estimate as well as insufficient or excess materials being ordered. It could also delay the remodeling and prove more expensive. Joellen decides that another alternative is to schedule another visit to the house to confirm the information in her notes. She contacts the client and returns to the house where she remeasures the windows and determines that her original notes were incorrect. As she remembered, one window is indeed larger than the other two.

Remember!

Interact Effectively with Others At the end of a conversation with a client or coworker, it is a good idea to summarize any decisions that were made during the conversation. This will confirm that you understand what was said and what is expected. If Joellen had done this, she would have identified and corrected her error at her initial visit. She would not have needed to follow up with the client.

Detecting Errors Aaron is the office manager for a software developer. Part of his job is faxing supply orders from company departments to supply vendors. He prepares to fax an order when he notices that information looks incorrect.

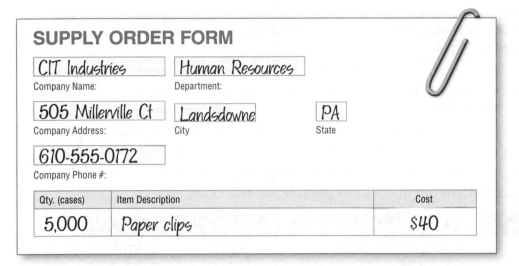

SUPPLY ORDER FORM

CIT Industries	Human Resources	
Company Name:	Department:	

505 Millerville Ct	Landsdowne	PA
Company Address:	City	State

610-555-0172
Company Phone #:

Qty. (cases)	Item Description	Cost
5,000	Paper clips	$40

The form indicates that the human resources (HR) department wants to order 5,000 cases of paper clips. Aaron wonders if that amount is correct. The HR manager has left for the day, so Aaron cannot verify the information. He sends the order form to the supplier.

1. Which of the following is a potential consequence of Aaron's actions?

   A. The HR department may receive a larger order than it needed.

   B. The HR department may receive a smaller order than it needed.

   C. The HR manager will be upset that Aaron spent the department's entire supply budget on paper clips.

   D. The HR manager will no longer have Aaron fax orders.

   E. The HR manager will be fired for wasting company money.

2. What should Aaron have done differently to make sure he ordered the correct amount of supplies?

   F. waited to order the supplies until the information was verified

   G. told the HR manager to stay at the office until the order form was faxed

   H. been present when the HR manager filled in the form

   J. sent the HR manager an e-mail accusing her of wasting company money

   K. asked his supervisor if the information was correct

Reflect In each of the *Try It Out!* examples, Joellen and Aaron needed to verify information before they could complete their tasks. What could each of them have done to prevent the errors from occurring in the first place? What other choices could they have made to fix the problems? What might the consequences of those actions have been?

On Your Own ▪ ▪ ▪

Read the following scenarios. Then answer the questions that follow each scenario.

SCENARIO A Obtaining Information

You are a limousine driver for a five star hotel. Most of the hotel's guests come from out of town. Therefore, a large part of your work involves picking up and dropping off customers at the airport.

> Your limousine dispatcher in the office assigns you to pick up a new customer at the airport. As you park, you realize that you have left your pick-up paperwork at the office. You do not remember the name of the client. You usually write the client's name on a sign so the client can identify you when he or she de-planes.

Complete the chart below and then answer the questions that follow.

Decision-Making Process				
STEP 1: Identify the Problem	**STEP 2:** Locate, Gather, and Organize Relevant Information	**STEP 3:** Generate Alternatives	**STEP 4:** Choose a Solution	**STEP 5:** Implement the Solution
You are at the airport to pick up a client, but do not know the client's name.	Your limousine dispatcher is in the office. You need the client's name so he or she can locate you in a crowd.			

1. What are some alternative solutions that you can take to resolve this problem?

2. Which solution would you choose to implement? What are the consequences of this solution?

SCENARIO B Detecting Errors

You work for a laboratory supply company. Part of your job as an accounts manager is to process order forms. After you confirm that an order form has all the necessary information, you send it to the packaging and shipping department.

> You are in the process of reviewing a form. You realize that the form contains an incorrect total for the price. However, all of the shipping information is correct. You also know that all of the requested items are available.

3. What is the problem that you need to solve?

4. What might the consequences be if you forward the form as it currently appears?

SCENARIO C Completing Forms

You are an insurance claims adjuster. You have just interviewed a person who was in a car accident. You need to transfer information from your notes onto the proper form.

Name: J. Maldonado
Account #: 132-887-00034
Description: Lost control
around a curve, hit a tree
Did not file report with police

AUTO CLAIM FORM

Driver: Maldonado, J.

Acct#: 132-887-00034

Passengers Y/N

Injuries Reported Y/N

Description of Incident:

Lost control around a curve, hit a tree

Police Report Filed Y/N No

5. What information needs to be added in order to correctly complete the form?

6. Whom should you contact to identify any missing information?

SCENARIO D Maintaining Logs

You work as a manager for a convenience store. Your dairy deliveries should have arrived this morning, but the shelves are bare. You check the delivery log.

DELIVERY LOG

Name of Driver	Date of Delivery	Items Delivered	Delivered Where?
Greg	May 14th	40 pints half-n-half	Storage cooler
Stacey	May 21st	20 pints cream	Sent back to distributor—
		6 gallons 2% milk	cooler locked.

7. What information in the delivery log tells you why the shelves are bare?

8. What are potential solutions to this problem? What are the consequences?

Summary ▪ ▪ ▪

When you submit or receive information, check for accuracy by doing the following:

- **Complete forms and maintain logs** Enter information clearly, completely, and correctly. Others rely on these forms to help them do their jobs.

- **Detect errors** Take responsibility by notifying the person who made an error and do what you can to help correct the problem.

- **Obtain information** Ask others to verify incomplete or confusing information.

Answers begin on page 124.

Lesson 4
Customer Satisfaction

Customer service refers to services offered by a company to a client. By offering these services, the company hopes to keep its clients satisfied. People with good customer service skills understand customer needs and provide personalized service. They also act professionally and keep customers informed.

Skill Examples

Understanding Customer Needs Monique and Ronaldo both work as sales associates in retail stores. They often answer customers' questions about the items they sell.

Read the two examples and answer the questions that follow.

EXAMPLE 1 **Ronaldo's Customer**
Ronaldo works for a sporting goods store. A customer approaches him to ask where she can find a helmet for her daughter.

> *Hi! Can I help you find something? You're looking for a helmet for your daughter? Well, we have several different types. What sport will she be playing? Lacrosse? That's a great sport, and she will definitely need a helmet. Here's the section of lacrosse gear. The helmets are on the left. We have lots of different colors, but be sure you choose one that is the correct size. Here is a sizing chart for you to review before you make your selection.*

The customer chooses a helmet. The next week, she is back to purchase more lacrosse gear. She is able to head directly to the lacrosse section.

1. How do Ronaldo's actions show that he can provide personalized service?
   A. They show that he cares only about customers who are interested in lacrosse.
   B. They show that he is especially interested in selling helmets.
   C. They show that he does not sell helmets directly to children.
   D. They show that he asks questions to guide customers to the right product.
   E. They show that he wrote detailed sizing charts for his customers to review.

2. What would have happened if Ronaldo did not ask his customer any questions when she visited the store the first time?
   F. The customer may not have found exactly what she needed.
   G. The customer would have been impressed with Ronaldo's customer service skills.
   H. Ronaldo would have been able to direct her to what she was looking for in the store.
   J. Ronaldo would have had to call the customer to apologize.
   K. The customer would have found a lacrosse helmet more quickly.

Remember!

Serve Clients It is your responsibility to give customers accurate information to help them make decisions and meet their needs. If you are not sure about what a customer is asking for, be sure to ask clarifying questions. In *Example 1*, a customer asks Ronaldo for something general. By asking follow-up questions, Ronaldo can be sure he is selling the customer the right item.

Tools for Workplace Success

EXAMPLE 2 Monique's Customer

Monique works as a salesperson for a clothing store. The store specializes in selling jeans for different body types.

> A customer enters the store. She takes a look around and then walks up to talk to Monique. She asks Monique where to find women's jeans. Monique points to the back half of the store and says, "Women's jeans are on the back wall." The customer walks to the back, but sees dozens of different types of jeans on the back wall.

3. What might the consequences of Monique's actions be for her customer?

    A. The customer will know exactly where to find the right pair of jeans.

    B. The customer will spend a lot of time looking for the right pair of jeans.

    C. The customer will decide to buy a shirt as well as a pair of jeans.

    D. The customer will find a better pair of jeans in a different store.

    E. The customer will recommend the store to her friends.

4. What would probably have happened if Monique had asked the customer follow-up questions to help her find the right pair of jeans?

    F. The customer would have been upset with Monique for being nosy.

    G. The customer would not have found the jeans she wanted.

    H. The customer would have decided to buy shirts instead of jeans.

    J. The customer would have found the right pair of jeans more quickly.

    K. The customer would have given Monique wrong answers to mislead her.

Think About It Ronaldo and Monique both interact with customers regularly. What kind of impression do you think Ronaldo and Monique made on their customers? How did their actions affect the experience the customer had in their stores? In forming your answer, think about the following questions:

- **Commitment to Quality** How did Ronaldo and Monique make their customers feel welcomed and valued?

- **Communication** What did Ronaldo's and Monique's interactions with their customers say about their knowledge of the products at their stores?

Remember!

Know How to Learn

When you interact with customers and clients, you need to be knowledgeable about the products and services your company offers. You also need to share that information with your clients. This will help them find what they need. In *Example 2*, Monique failed to provide her customer with information that would help her make an informed purchase. As a result, Monique may have frustrated the customer and lost a possible sale.

Try It Out! ■ ■ ■

Providing Personalized Service Regina is the head chef at a catering hall. She and her kitchen staff are preparing for a wedding party of 100 guests.

> One day before the event, Regina's supervisor approaches her. He explains that one guest has a wheat allergy and cannot eat any foods that contain wheat. Regina will have to develop a special meal for this guest. Regina is frustrated. She has already planned the menu and purchased the ingredients. Her first course is a pasta dish, and many of the other courses include wheat ingredients.

Regina does not have a lot of time. Not only does she need to create new dishes for the wedding, but she will also need time to purchase ingredients if she does not have them at the catering hall. However, her employer is counting on her to prepare meals that each guest will enjoy.

Decision-Making Process				
STEP 1: Identify the Problem	**STEP 2:** Locate, Gather, and Organize Relevant Information	**STEP 3:** Generate Alternatives	**STEP 4:** Choose a Solution	**STEP 5:** Implement the Solution
Regina has to make extra dishes she did not prepare for ahead of time.	The new dishes require special preparation (no wheat). Regina does not have a lot of time. The catering hall is relying on Regina's talent as a chef.	Regina can tell the manager that it is too late for special requests. Regina can ask her kitchen staff to help her accommodate the late request.	She chooses to ask her kitchen staff to help her with these special meals.	Regina sends a kitchen staff member to the grocery store for some additional ingredients. She devises two additional entrees—both with no wheat.

Regina thought she had finalized the menu for the wedding. However, she did not realize that one of the guests had dietary restrictions. Identifying new dishes will require special thought and attention, and they will take additional time to make. Unfortunately, Regina does not have a lot of time. Her first option is to tell the manager that it is too late to add new dishes to the menu. Her other option is to discuss the issue with her kitchen staff and brainstorm ideas. Because the catering hall wants to satisfy each guest, Regina decides to discuss the issue with her staff. With the help of the kitchen staff, Regina comes up with two new dishes. She later hears that all of the guests were very pleased with their meals.

Acting Professionally Louis owns and manages a small florist shop. He is responsible for meeting with customers to discuss the flower arrangements they need for their events.

> Louis is working with a bride on final flower arrangements for her wedding. The wedding is just days away. The original order included 1,000 white roses for the bouquets and centerpieces. However, the bride now asks if the order for white roses can be doubled to 2,000 flowers. Louis is not able to order that many extra roses on such short notice. The bride becomes very angry and demands that Louis find a way to get her more white roses.

Louis tries to explain to the bride that he cannot guarantee an extra 1,000 roses by her wedding day. She is still angry. Louis also gets upset. He tells her she should have thought about the additional flowers sooner.

1. Which of the following is a potential consequence of Louis' actions?
    A. The bride will decide to postpone the wedding until the flowers are available.
    B. The bride will calm down and understand that she was unreasonable.
    C. The bride will tell her friends and family not to do business at Louis' shop.
    D. The bride will change her request from roses to daisies.
    E. The bride will praise Louis for his excellent customer service.

2. What could Louis have done differently to improve the situation?
    F. He could have told the bride he would order the flowers, even though they would not arrive in time for the wedding.
    G. He could have refused to work with the bride due to her unreasonable requests.
    H. He could have offered to check if other florists had white roses available.
    J. He could have explained that the wholesaler he orders from is out of white roses.
    K. He could have told the bride only red roses are available.

Reflect In each of the *Try It Out!* examples, Regina and Louis had to help customers with special requests. Regina chose to discuss a way to meet the customer's request with her team. This helped her come up with a solution that allowed her to fulfill the special request and make the customer happy. When Louis realized he could not fulfill his customer's exact request, he could have presented her with other options. Instead, by losing his temper, he damaged his professional relationship with her and could lose her business. He could also lose potential business since the bride might have recommended him to others. Did each person take the right steps to overcome his or her problems? What were the positive and negative effects of their actions?

Remember!

Resolve Conflict and Negotiate Sometimes you will not be able to fulfill your customer's specific request. In these situations, try to suggest another option. For example, Louis could have provided alternatives to the bride. He could have suggested using another flower in the same color.

On Your Own ■ ■ ■

Read the following scenarios. Then answer the questions that follow each scenario.

SCENARIO A Keeping Customers Informed

You are a plumber for a large contractor. This week you have been working on remodeling a bathroom. So far everything has been on schedule.

> Yesterday, you removed all the old fixtures from the bathroom. The new fixtures were supposed to be shipped to the client's home so you could install them today. When you arrive in the morning, the fixtures are not there. You call the company that was supposed to ship the fixtures. They tell you the fixtures are on the way, but they may not be delivered until the evening. The client does not want you working in his home late in the evening.

Complete the chart below and then answer the questions that follow.

Decision-Making Process				
STEP 1: Identify the Problem	**STEP 2:** Locate, Gather, and Organize Relevant Information	**STEP 3:** Generate Alternatives	**STEP 4:** Choose a Solution	**STEP 5:** Implement the Solution
You need to install new fixtures for a client, but the fixtures have not arrived yet.	The fixtures may not arrive until evening. The client does not want you working in his home late in the evening.			

1. What are some alternative ways to solve this problem?

2. What solution will allow you to keep the client's needs in mind?

3. To whom would you need to communicate your solution? How would you do so?

SCENARIO B Understanding Customer Needs

You own a rental shop for power tools. Part of your duties include reviewing orders that were placed online.

> While reviewing an online order, you notice that the customer requested a handheld blower for a landscaping job. You know that you have a backpack blower that would be much better for the work the customer described, but it is slightly more expensive.

4. What are your options regarding how to respond to your customer?

5. What are the likely consequences of implementing these options?

SCENARIO C Acting Professionally

As a gate agent at a busy airport, you are assigned to take tickets. You have just learned that a fully booked flight is being delayed due to inclement weather.

> Some passengers are concerned that they will miss their connecting flights in the destination city. You know that your airline has a policy of rescheduling connecting flights due to weather delays. The passengers are becoming impatient. An upset customer approaches you and starts raising his voice.

6. What are the different ways you could respond to the upset customer?

7. Which response would you choose to assist the customer?

8. What are the consequences of your response?

SCENARIO D Providing Personalized Service

Part of your new job as a hotel desk clerk involves responding to guests' questions and requests. You have recently checked in a guest staying at the hotel on a business trip.

> After settling in his room, the guest phones the front desk. He tells you that the television in his room is not working. He would like you to send someone up to his room to fix the television or replace it. You know that the hotel does not have extra televisions. You are not sure if someone working can fix the problem.

9. What is the problem that you need to find a solution for?

10. If no one can fix the television, what alternative solutions can you propose?

11. What are the potential consequences of the alternate solutions?

Summary ▪ ▪ ▪

Customers remember good service and tend to be loyal to companies that treat them with respect. To develop good customer service skills, be sure to do the following:

- **Understand customer needs** Ask relevant questions and pay attention to the details of the answers you receive.

- **Provide personalized service** It can be easy to treat a customer as just another person in line. Remember that each person you serve is an individual.

- **Act professionally** If a customer becomes angry or frustrated, continue to act professionally and treat the customer with respect.

- **Keep customers informed** Always keep customers informed of any changes, problems, or information that may impact them.

Answers begin on page 124.

Working with Others ...

The ability to work with diverse people is an important part of most jobs. You need to be positive in your actions, accepting of differences, and sensitive to others' needs. Creating and maintaining good working relationships will make you more effective in your job and more valued as an employee.

In Theme 2, you will learn about skills and behaviors that will help you work effectively with others.

Lesson 5: Interacting with Others Working in diverse workplaces creates opportunities to develop knowledge, positivity, and sensitivity. *Objectives include*:

- Working with Diverse People
- Demonstrating Insight into Behavior
- Demonstrating Sensitivity/Empathy
- Offering/Responding to Criticism
- Maintaining Open Relationships
- Learning about Other Cultures

Lesson 6: Active Listening Being an active listener means paying attention to details and appreciating the speaker's concerns and feelings. *Objectives include:*

- Identifying Important Information
- Paying Attention, Comprehending, and Responding
- Understanding Complex Instructions
- Appreciating Feelings and Concerns

Lesson 7: Effective Speaking Employees who communicate clearly, consistently, and persuasively express their ideas effectively. *Objectives include*:

- Recognizing and Using Nonverbal Expression
- Using Logical Organization
- Using Persuasive Language
- Understanding the Audience and the Nature of Information
- Using Common English Conventions

Lesson 8: Working Together Cooperation creates productive relationships among team members and employees. *Objectives include*:

- Identifying with the Team and Its Goals
- Acknowledging Team Membership and Roles
- Establishing Productive Relationships
- Resolving Conflicts

Key Factors for Working with Others ▪ ▪ ▪

These lessons are intended to help you identify and practice behaviors necessary for working with others. Interacting effectively with others is essential for maximizing your performance. In most professions, you are required to work and interact with others in person, on the telephone, or through e-mail. To effectively and consistently work with others, you must be able to:

- **Resolve conflict and negotiate** Recognizing problems and constructively working through them is part of being an effective team member. Maintaining positive relationships will help you and your company achieve your goals.

- **Be sociable** Communicating effectively with employees is crucial to individual and team success. Open and honest communication helps establish a positive and productive work environment.

- **Be flexible** Flexible employees are able to adapt to changing situations. Being able to handle various environments and people is necessary for success.

By knowing how to work with others, you can demonstrate an ability to build effective relationships with diverse people. Employers look for employees with this trait because it is essential for success.

Lesson 5
Interacting with Others

No matter where you work, you will need to interact with diverse people. You should be willing to learn about their cultures. When working with others, it is also important to be positive when offering or responding to criticism, to accept their concerns with empathy and sensitivity, and to be insightful in meeting their needs. This way you will create a good working relationship with them.

Skill Examples

Working with Diverse People Maria and Bill are cooks at a pizzeria. They would both like to take the following Tuesday off for personal reasons.

Read the two examples and answer the questions that follow.

EXAMPLE 1 Maria's Request for Time Off

> Maria is a cook at a pizzeria. She is reliable and enjoys the work she does. Maria is also a single parent, so sometimes she has to take time off to care for her son. Today, Maria asks her supervisor for next Tuesday off so she can take her son to the doctor for a checkup. Maria's supervisor tells her she cannot have Tuesday off. Another employee has already requested that day off to observe a religious holiday. Maria nods in understanding and asks if she may have Wednesday off. Her second request is approved.

1. How do Maria's actions show that she respects diversity in the workplace?
   A. By accepting her supervisor's response, she shows that she understands and accepts the culture and beliefs of her coworker.
   B. By asking for Wednesday off, she allows other employees to take on more hours.
   C. By approaching her supervisor for the day off, she shows that she respects authority figures.
   D. By becoming angry at her supervisor, she asserts her independence in the workplace.
   E. By becoming visibly upset, she is able to convince her coworker to come in on Tuesday.

2. How do you think Maria's coworker would react if Maria told him that he needed to work on his holiday so that she could take the day off?
   F. He would suggest that they both take the day off.
   G. He would approach the supervisor to ask for Wednesday off instead.
   H. He would be offended by Maria's lack of respect for his religious beliefs.
   J. He would ask Maria to attend religious services with him on Tuesday.
   K. He would reconsider taking the day off so Maria could take her son to the doctor.

Remember!

Solve Problems and Make Decisions When diverse groups of people work together, conflicts may arise based on differences in culture. It is important to be respectful of these differences while working together to resolve the conflict. In *Example 1,* when Maria's supervisor denies her request for Tuesday off, Maria does not get angry or ignore her obligation to take her son to the doctor. Instead, she comes up with an alternative solution—taking off another day. Maria's supervisor is likely to appreciate her flexibility and her problem-solving ability.

Tools for Workplace Success

EXAMPLE 2 Bill's Request for Time Off

> Bill is a cook at the same pizzeria as Maria. Bill was also hoping to take Tuesday off, since he has friends in town and would like to spend more time with them. Bill approaches his supervisor with his request, but he is denied. His supervisor mentions that another employee has already received the day off for a religious holiday. Bill is angry at this response. He complains to another employee that he deserves to have that day off because he is a good worker and mentions that he has never even heard of the religious holiday.

3. What might happen as a result of Bill's reaction to not receiving the day off?

   A. He might be forced to attend religious services with his coworker.

   B. He might have to work on Tuesday and Wednesday.

   C. He might earn a reputation for being intolerant of others.

   D. He might make friends with other employees who do not like their supervisor.

   E. He might convince his supervisor to give him Tuesday off.

4. What would have happened if Bill had responded by asking for a different day off instead?

   F. He would have shown that he was not sensitive to diversity.

   G. He would have been respectful of his coworker's needs and still gotten a day off.

   H. His supervisor would have given him Tuesday off anyway.

   J. His coworker would have stopped practicing his religious faith during the workweek.

   K. He would have earned a reputation for being a pushover.

Think About It Think about how Maria and Bill responded to their situations. How do you think they will be perceived by their supervisors and coworkers based on their actions? If you were the coworker who needed a day off for a religious holiday and you overheard Bill's comment, how would you feel the next time you had to work alongside him? In forming your answer, think about the following questions:

- **Resolve Conflict and Negotiate** How did Maria negotiate to meet her own needs as well as those of her supervisor and her coworker? What could Bill have done differently to negotiate with his supervisor?

- **Cooperate with Others** Bill and Maria both had to find a way to meet their own needs while also respecting the needs of others. Was either Bill or Maria successful in working with others?

Remember!

Resolve Conflict and Negotiate In *Example 2,* Bill could have shown his respect for his coworker's diversity by adapting his needs and working to positively resolve the scheduling conflict. Understanding and tolerance are important when addressing differences in religion as well as in age and gender.

Try It Out! ■ ■ ■

Demonstrating Insight into Behavior Ricardo is a call center supervisor for a telemarketing company. One of Ricardo's main responsibilities is to listen in on calls and make sure the telemarketers on his staff follow all the company guidelines during the calls. Today, Ricardo is listening in on a call when he hears the following:

> *Yes, sir. I have already spoken to you twice today. I understand you are frustrated. However, we have a very strict return policy. I explained the policy to you during our last phone call. I apologize, but there is nothing more I can do for you. Hello? Hello? You hung up? What a jerk!*

When the call is complete, Ricardo knows he needs to discuss the event with his employee. This employee does not have a history of getting angry on the phone, so Ricardo is not sure why the employee became frustrated during this call. He decides it is important to find out the details.

Decision-Making Process

STEP 1: Identify the Problem	STEP 2: Locate, Gather, and Organize Relevant Information	STEP 3: Generate Alternatives	STEP 4: Choose a Solution	STEP 5: Implement the Solution
Ricardo knows his employee became frustrated during a call but is not sure why.	Ricardo knows his employee became frustrated during a call. Ricardo knows this employee does not have a history of getting angry on the phone.	Ricardo can reprimand the employee and send her home. Ricardo can question the employee to learn more about her frustrations.	Ricardo does not want to appear "soft," but he also does not want to overreact. He chooses to give the employee a chance to explain herself before deciding if a reprimand is necessary.	Ricardo asks the employee to meet with him. He replays the call for her to hear and asks her why she made the negative remark.

Ricardo gives the employee a chance to explain her actions. He finds out that during a previous exchange, the caller had used profane language while on the phone. The employee felt hurt and offended, since she was only following company policies and trying her best. Ricardo understands that sometimes the workplace becomes stressful, but he also knows that the employee behaved inappropriately. He issues her a verbal warning to be sure to keep her emotions under control on the phone in the future. He also encourages her to speak to a member of the management team about these types of difficult situations before getting to the point of anger or frustration on the phone.

Remember!

Cooperating with Others Both supervisors and employees sometimes experience stress in the workplace. When you openly and honestly express your concerns and frustrations to your supervisor, you may find that he or she has solutions you might not have considered. He or she is likely to have had experiences similar to yours in the past. Ricardo had experienced frustrating phone calls as a former telemarketer. He knew that his employee might have benefited from speaking to a member of the management team before she got to the point of expressing her anger on the phone.

Demonstrating Sensitivity/Empathy Melissa works at a bank that takes calls from customers who want to apply for instant automobile loans over the phone. Because many of the callers do not qualify for the loans, Melissa often has to break bad news to her customers. Today, Melissa is on the phone with a caller.

> *Hello, Mr. Davidson. I have just received the results of your automobile loan application. Unfortunately, you were not approved… Yes, sir, that is our final decision… No, sir, unfortunately our policy requires a 30-day period before you can reapply… Sir, my supervisor will tell you the same thing… Sir, I will not allow you to speak to anyone else. My supervisor is busy, and besides, there's nothing she can do for you… I talk to people like you all the time. You're just like all the others who did not qualify for a loan— irresponsible with money, and now you want me to fix all your problems for you. There's nothing I can do. Goodbye.*

Melissa's call was overheard by a supervisor. She is immediately called into a meeting. During the meeting she is formally reprimanded for insensitivity toward the customer on the phone. Melissa is confused and upset. As she mentioned on the phone, there was nothing she could do for the customer since he did not qualify for the loan. Company policy does not allow anyone to reapply for 30 days. Melissa thinks she did the right thing by being honest with the caller.

1. Which of these best explains why Melissa was reprimanded?
   A. She told the customer he could not reapply for the loan for 30 days.
   B. She told the customer she would let him reapply in two weeks.
   C. She did not address the customer politely by calling him "Sir."
   D. She hung up on the customer before explaining the reapplication policy.
   E. She made an insensitive comment about the customer's financial situation.

2. If Melissa handled the call with more sensitivity, which of these would be most likely to occur?
   F. The customer might still be upset, but Melissa's supervisor would be pleased with her actions.
   G. Melissa's supervisor would have allowed the customer to reapply for a loan.
   H. Melissa would have made the customer happy, but would have angered her supervisor.
   J. The customer would have called Melissa's supervisor to complain.
   K. Melissa would have convinced her company to change the 30-day policy.

Reflect In both of the *Try It Out!* examples, the employees used their interpersonal skills to decide what course of action to take. In what ways did Ricardo use his insight into behavior to resolve conflict with his employee? In what ways did Melissa show a lack of sensitivity in her attempt to resolve conflict with her caller?

Remember!

Customer Relations

In many careers, workers must be responsible for delivering bad news to customers, patients, or clients. It is important to remain professional and demonstrate sensitivity even if the customer, patient, or client reacts rudely to the bad news. Workers with good interpersonal skills have good relationships with customers and attract other customers. Melissa may not have been able to avoid delivering bad news to the caller. However, she could have demonstrated integrity by remaining professional and polite even if the customer became pushy on the phone.

On Your Own ▪ ▪ ▪

Read the following scenarios. Then answer the questions that follow each scenario.

SCENARIO A Working with Diverse People
In addition to your normal tasks as a medical assistant, you have been asked to help train a new medical assistant who is an older woman.

> Your manager has asked you to train a new medical assistant. She is older, and you are worried that she may struggle to learn your office's software system. It took you three days to learn it. She is comfortable with basic computer skills, but seems to be having difficulty learning the patient entry system.

Complete the chart below and then answer the questions that follow.

Decision-Making Process				
STEP 1: Identify the Problem	**STEP 2:** Locate, Gather, and Organize Relevant Information	**STEP 3:** Generate Alternatives	**STEP 4:** Choose a Solution	**STEP 5:** Implement the Solution
The new employee is comfortable with computers but is having trouble with the office software.	The woman is comfortable with basic computer skills. You took three days to learn the system.			

1. What solution did you choose to implement for this problem?

2. How will the solution you chose help you and the new employee begin a positive working relationship?

SCENARIO B Offering/Responding to Criticism
You work at the post office sorting mail. On some days, such as workdays near major holidays, you have to sort more mail than usual, and this causes stress.

> On a stressful day, your supervisor snaps at you for not working fast enough. You think your productivity is normal compared to other days. You take a look at the amount of work you have remaining and are confident you will be able to complete all your tasks before the end of the day.

3. Why do you think your supervisor seems so frustrated?

4. What solutions could you suggest to your supervisor to ease her stress?

5. How would you react if your supervisor refuses to accept your solutions and continues to blame your work performance for the difficulties she is having today?

SCENARIO C Maintaining Open Relationships

As the night-shift manager for a restaurant, you manage the restaurant staff during the busiest time of the day.

> After discussing the menu specials of the day with the staff, you go into your office to focus on some paperwork until the dinner crowd arrives. You have a lot of paperwork to complete before the first dinner guests arrive. You sometimes get annoyed when people knock on the door to ask questions.

6. What problems might your routine of working in your office before dinner service cause?

7. What could you do to create and maintain an open relationship with your staff?

SCENARIO D Learning about Other Cultures

You work for a housekeeping company that services office buildings after hours.

> You have just been promoted to team leader, and you are about to arrive on-site with a new team. You are excited to begin working with new team members, but you are also intimidated. You have never managed other people before, and you know that your new team is a very diverse group of people.

8. What challenges do you face as the new manager of a diverse group of people?

9. What strategies could you use to connect with each team member?

Summary ▪ ▪ ▪

Employees with good interpersonal skills are the type of people others want to work with. To ensure that you have good interpersonal skills, be sure to do the following:

- **Be aware of diversity** Recognize that people come from diverse backgrounds.

- **Demonstrate sensitivity and empathy** Be supportive if a coworker, supervisor, or employee is having a difficult day.

- **Demonstrate insight** Pay attention to what coworkers are saying and doing, and offer to help if you see that someone appears to have a problem.

- **Maintain open relationships** Make sure others know that you are willing to listen and help in the workplace.

- **Learn about other cultures** Inform yourself about the diverse needs and values of your coworkers.

- **Offer and respond to criticism** Do not make or take criticism personally. Be positive and believe that your coworker is trying to do the best he or she can.

Answers begin on page 126.

Lesson 6 ■ ■ ■
Active Listening

Being a good listener involves more than just staying quiet until it is your turn to speak. Good listeners pay attention to the details of what they are hearing. You must be able to consider what others are saying to you and identify important information. You also need to show an appreciation of other people's feelings and concerns. These skills will make you a better, more trusted employee.

Skill Examples ■ ■ ■

Identifying Important Information Toni and Darryl are both caterers. They each have a meeting with a new client this afternoon.

Read the two examples and answer the questions that follow.

EXAMPLE 1 Toni's Client Interview

> Toni works as a caterer. An important part of her job involves talking to clients. When she meets with clients, Toni has to keep track of many important details. These include the time and date of the event, the number of people who will attend, the kinds of food the clients like best, and whether any of the guests have dietary restrictions. Because Toni needs to remember so many important details, she always brings a notebook when she meets with clients. Today, her client meeting goes well. When Toni gets back to her kitchen, she reviews her notes and makes sure to enter the date and time of the event on her computer's calendar.

1. Based on Toni's actions, why might her client perceive her as having good listening skills?
   A. She arrives early to the interview and introduces herself enthusiastically.
   B. She arrives late to the interview to show the client how busy she is.
   C. She always wears chef coats so clients will take her seriously.
   D. She hides her notebook under the table so the client will not think she has a bad memory.
   E. She identifies the important information about her client's event.

2. What would be a possible consequence if Toni did not pay attention to everything that her client had to say?
   F. Toni would remember all the details about the event.
   G. Toni would take excellent notes.
   H. Toni would miss important information about the event.
   J. Toni would leave the meeting feeling confident about her ability to meet all of the client's needs.
   K. Toni would impress the client with her listening skills.

Remember!

Listening Actively Good listeners pay attention and identify important details so they can meet the needs of coworkers and clients. In *Example 1,* even though Toni remembers to bring her notebook, she still needs to pay attention in order to be a good listener. She needs to listen for important details, such as the time and date of the event. If she does not retain these details, she may forget to include them in her notes.

Tools for Workplace Success

EXAMPLE 2 Darryl's Client Interview

Darryl is a head caterer at a large catering company. Darryl often meets with several clients a day. Today, he is meeting a client about an event. This is the third meeting Darryl has attended today, and he is tired from his previous meetings. When the client arrives at Darryl's catering hall, Darryl begins to talk to the client about the details of the event. Darryl asks many good questions, such as the time and date of the event and the number of people who will attend, and he describes the various food options available. Because he is tired, however, he does not pay attention when the client describes the guests' dietary restrictions. At the end of the meeting, Darryl feels he has a good idea of what the client needs. Later that day, as Darryl is putting together a schedule for the next month, he realizes that he does not know if any of the guests are vegetarians or if any of them have food allergies.

3. Based on Darryl's actions, why might his client perceive him as having good listening skills?

   A. He asks many good questions about the details of his client's event.

   B. He meets with more than one client each day.

   C. He meets with clients at the catering hall rather than at their homes.

   D. He describes the various food options available for the event.

   E. He puts together his schedule one month in advance of an event.

4. If Darryl has to call a client back to confirm basic information, how do you think the client will view Darryl?

   F. The client will think Darryl is very attentive to details.

   G. The client will think Darryl did a poor job of paying attention to his needs at their meeting.

   H. The client will think Darryl is an excellent caterer.

   J. The client will think Darryl is trying to reschedule the event.

   K. The client will expect Darryl to give him a discount.

Think About It Think about the different ways in which Toni and Darryl planned for their client meetings. Client meetings are intended for the caterer to learn more about the client's needs. How would you feel if you were in a meeting with a caterer like Toni? How did Darryl's actions before and after the meeting affect his opportunity to impress the client? In forming your answer, think about the following questions:

- **Listen Actively** What steps did Toni and Darryl take to make sure that they were able to listen actively to their clients and retain the important details? How did their actions affect their meetings?

- **Cooperate with Others** When clients meet with a caterer, they want to feel their events are important. In what ways did both Toni and Darryl express interest in their clients' events? How did the interviews differ?

Remember!

Responsibility

Whenever you are in a situation where you know you will need to remember a lot of information, be sure to give the conversation your full attention. People who are able to identify and retain important information are seen as good listeners and as people who can be trusted to follow directions. In *Example 1,* Toni identifies the important information from her meeting with the client and makes a good impression. In *Example 2,* Darryl is tired and does not give the meeting his full attention, so he misses important information. He will have to call the client again to ask for information that the client has already given him, demonstrating poor listening skills.

Try It Out! ■ ■ ■

Paying Attention, Comprehending, and Responding Carly is a veterinary technician at an animal hospital. The veterinarians at the hospital rely on Carly to complete tasks that they are too busy to do.

> Carly's supervisor, the veterinarian on duty, has asked her to explain the follow-up care to a customer who is picking up her sick cat. The veterinarian explains the follow-up care to Carly and then leaves to see another patient. Carly walks to the examination room to talk to the customer. However, just before entering the room, she realizes that she is unclear about some of the details of the follow-up care. She thinks she knows how the cat's medication should be administered but is not sure.

Carly knows that good follow-up care is essential to making a sick animal better. She also knows that if she gives incorrect information, she might be held responsible if the cat gets sicker after it goes home.

Decision-Making Process				
STEP 1: Identify the Problem	**STEP 2:** Locate, Gather, and Organize Relevant Information	**STEP 3:** Generate Alternatives	**STEP 4:** Choose a Solution	**STEP 5:** Implement the Solution
Carly needs to explain follow-up care to a customer but is unclear about some of the details.	Carly knows good follow-up care is very important. Carly knows the customer will follow her instructions, even if her instructions are incorrect.	Carly can tell the customer what she thinks the instructions are. Carly can tell the veterinarian that she is unclear about some of the details and ask for clarification.	She chooses to ask for clarification from the veterinarian before talking to the customer.	Carly gets clarification from the veterinarian before she explains the instructions to the customer.

Part of listening well is making sure you understand everything. It is better to ask questions than to guess or remain unclear. Carly recognizes that she made a mistake by not making sure she was clear about all the details of the follow-up care before the end of her conversation with the veterinarian. She takes initiative to correct her error by asking the veterinarian to clarify some details. When Carly asks for clarification, she shows that she wants to make sure she has the correct information and understands what is expected from her. She also shows that she can be relied upon to make good decisions and take responsibility for her actions.

Remember!

Self-Management

When you are responsible for giving others critical information, it is very important that you make sure you are confident in your message before you give it. Pay attention to the information relayed to you. Make sure you understand all of the details and ask for clarification if necessary. Respond to the speaker to indicate that you understand or to ask any questions you may have. Carly shows good self-management skills by choosing to verify her message before speaking to the client.

Understanding Complex Instructions Kelsey has just been hired as a security guard for a government building. He will be working the night shift, when much of the building is empty. Kelsey knows that he will spend a large part of his shift by himself.

> When Kelsey arrives for his first shift, he is paired up with a coworker who will train him for an hour. After that hour, Kelsey will be left to oversee the building by himself for the rest of his shift. Kelsey's coworker suggests that, since the night shift tends to be pretty quiet, Kelsey spend his time walking around the building to learn where everything is located. The coworker then quickly explains the process for locking the interior doors, which he says is very important. Some doors must be locked using a code, others use a key, and some doors are left unlocked.

Kelsey's coworker leaves for the night, and Kelsey patrols the building. When it is time to lock the interior doors, he cannot remember each step of the process as his coworker explained it, so he leaves all of the interior doors unlocked.

1. How might Kelsey's actions influence his supervisor's opinion of him?
   A. His supervisor might be pleased that Kelsey patrolled the building.
   B. His supervisor might be frustrated that Kelsey did not patrol the building as instructed.
   C. His supervisor might be angry that the correct procedure was not followed.
   D. His supervisor might be glad that Kelsey did not bother any other employees.
   E. His supervisor might be disappointed that Kelsey will have to be fired because he did not follow procedures.

2. What could Kelsey have done to avoid the problem?
   F. He could have asked questions for clarification.
   G. He could have not paid attention to his coworker's explanation.
   H. He could have locked all of the doors.
   J. He could have asked his coworker to stay with him for his entire shift.
   K. He could have told his coworker that he understood how to lock the interior doors.

Reflect In both of the *Try It Out!* examples, the employees needed to understand important details to complete their assignments but did not understand the details that were given to them. What information did Carly and Kelsey use to make their decisions? What are some alternative actions they could have taken? What might the consequences of those actions have been?

Remember!

Integrity Even the best employees make mistakes sometimes. People may make mistakes because they did not pay attention to the details of an assignment or because the instructions were too complicated. If you find that you do not understand something, ask for clarification. If you do make a mistake, do not hide it. Demonstrate integrity by promptly asking your supervisor for assistance. Kelsey may not want to look confused, but it is better for him to ask for clarification than to leave the doors unlocked.

On Your Own ▪ ▪ ▪

Read the following scenarios. Then answer the questions that follow each scenario.

SCENARIO A Understanding Complex Instructions

You just started as an insurance processor in a doctor's office. One of your duties is to inform patients of rejected insurance claims. Your supervisor gives you instructions.

> *Instead of calling patients about rejected claims, we're going to start sending letters. So, you need to access the patient's electronic file, find the rejection form, fill in the required information, save the file, and then print it. Please pick up the form immediately from the printer to preserve our patients' privacy.*

You have over twenty letters to send. According to your supervisor, you need to pick up each printout from the printer across the office. To save time, you want to retrieve all the documents at once, instead of going back and forth. However, sensitive information would be left on the printer.

Complete the chart below and then answer the questions that follow.

Decision-Making Process				
STEP 1: Identify the Problem	**STEP 2:** Locate, Gather, and Organize Relevant Information	**STEP 3:** Generate Alternatives	**STEP 4:** Choose a Solution	**STEP 5:** Implement the Solution
You do not want to keep going to the printer, but you need to preserve patient privacy.	The printer is far away. The forms contain sensitive information.			

1. How did you decide which solution to choose?

2. After the task is complete, how could you verify that it was done correctly?

SCENARIO B Appreciating Feelings and Concerns

You work as a front-desk services representative for a busy, upscale hotel.

> A customer approaches you. He begins to complain about his room, telling you that he requested a room with a better view months ago. You try to pay attention, but you are trying to input another customer's reservation. The customer notices that you are not paying attention. He becomes even angrier.

3. What is the main problem with this interaction from the customer's point of view?

4. What steps could you take to make this customer's experience better and make sure his concerns are addressed?

SCENARIO C Identifying Important Information

As a moderator for a marketing company, part of your job is to lead focus groups—groups of people who try a product that is being developed and offer their opinions.

> You are leading a focus group that is discussing a new product. You assume you should only be concerned with identifying who is likely to purchase the new product. Only one member of the group thinks the product is very good, so you only pay close attention to this person. Other group members get annoyed that you are not listening to their suggestions for improving the product.

5. What problems might arise from only focusing on one participant's comments?

6. What actions could you take to solve this problem?

SCENARIO D Paying Attention, Comprehending, and Responding

You are a clerk in a bookstore, and one of your duties is to shelve new books. As you are signing in for your evening shift, your supervisor walks up to you. She gives you the following assignment.

> *Hi! There's a lot to do tonight. We just got this week's best-seller list, so please reorganize the best-seller section. Also, the book signing is tomorrow. Please create a special display for it up front. Thanks!*

Because you were signing in while your supervisor was talking, you did not give her your full attention. The next day, your supervisor is annoyed. She tells you that instead of creating a book-signing display up front, you created a best-seller display.

7. What problem could result from your not completing your task correctly?

8. What could you have done differently to avoid the problem?

Summary ▪ ▪ ▪

Employees who have good listening skills can be relied on to get the job done. To start developing good listening skills in the workplace, be sure to do the following:

- **Pay attention** When you are receiving instructions, pay close attention to them.

- **Identify important information** Take notes so you do not forget important details. If you are not sure whether a detail is important, ask about it.

- **Understand complex instructions** Some processes take a while to learn. It is okay to ask questions if you are not sure how to complete a task.

- **Appreciate feelings and concerns** Other people will notice and get offended if you are not really listening to them. Appreciate other people's need to be heard.

Answers begin on page 126.

Lesson 7 ■ ■ ■
Effective Speaking

Effective speakers communicate clearly. This is important because when you speak, you want to make sure your ideas are understood. To speak effectively, you must understand whom you are talking to and express information clearly, consistently, and persuasively. You have to be organized and speak with common English conventions. You also have to recognize and use nonverbal expression.

Skill Examples ■ ■ ■

Recognizing and Using Nonverbal Expression Leila and Omar both work in retail jobs where they must talk to customers on a daily basis.

Read the two examples and answer the questions that follow.

EXAMPLE 1 Leila's Sales Pitch

Leila works as a salesperson for an appliance manufacturer that wants to begin providing appliances to area hotels. Leila's supervisor has asked her to give a sales pitch to a hotel manager.

> *Hello, nice to meet you. I'm here to explain the many benefits of our appliances. We offer different kinds of appliances, a range of prices, and good services. If you want to come in to the office one day, I could show you some brochures that tell you all about each appliance's features.*

As Leila gives her sales pitch, she repeatedly looks down at the floor. She feels unsure what to do with her hands, so she folds her arms across her chest. The hotel manager politely declines her offer.

1. What might the client think about Leila based on her nonverbal cues?
   A. She seems uncomfortable speaking about her company's products.
   B. She seems enthusiastic about her company's products.
   C. She seems comfortable offering information.
   D. She seems aggravated by having to give a sales pitch about appliances.
   E. She seems well-prepared to give a sales pitch about appliances.

2. How might the hotel manager have responded to Leila's sales pitch if she had included several details about the products and services offered by her company and maintained eye contact throughout her presentation?
   F. The hotel manager would have criticized Leila for talking too much.
   G. The hotel manager would have been more interested in Leila's offer.
   H. The hotel manager would have remembered all the different appliances Leila's company manufactures.
   J. The hotel manager would have told Leila to stop looking at him.
   K. The hotel manager would have asked for a discount on the appliances.

Remember!

Self-Management
Nonverbal cues are messages that you send to an audience without speaking. They include facial expressions, body language, and gestures. In *Example 1,* Leila looks down at the floor and folds her arms across her chest during her presentation. These actions show that she is not confident in herself or her presentation. This may be the reason the hotel manager declines her offer. To appear confident and to connect with your audience, make eye contact, smile, and sit or stand up straight.

EXAMPLE 2 Omar's Sales Pitch

Omar works as a cashier at the front counter of a bakery. People often come in to browse, and Omar must describe the different choices so people will be enticed to buy baked goods.

> Hi there! Are you looking for something for yourself or for a party? We have lots of different options. If you like cookies, we have over thirty different kinds! My favorites are the chocolate chip and the vanilla almond shortbread. You can pick and choose as many kinds as you'd like; we charge by the pound.

When Omar approaches customers, he smiles broadly and waves for them to come closer to the bakery counter. When he is talking to them, he maintains eye contact and points out certain items as he mentions them.

3. How might customers respond to Omar based on what he says and his nonverbal cues?

   A. They might think Omar is nervous.

   B. They might think Omar does not know about the cookies in his bakery.

   C. They might think Omar does not like the baked goods.

   D. They might become interested in buying the products.

   E. They might feel like their needs are being neglected.

4. If Omar had provided the customers with information but had not smiled and invited them closer or maintained eye contact, which of these might have happened?

   F. The customers might have bought cakes instead of the vanilla almond shortbread cookies.

   G. The customers might have felt unwelcome and left without buying anything.

   H. The customers might have thought Omar was very knowledgeable and friendly.

   J. The customers might have bought products that Omar did not recommend.

   K. The customers might have thought Omar was an enthusiastic salesperson.

Think About It Think about the verbal and nonverbal information Leila and Omar gave to their customers. How did their nonverbal cues differ? How did their verbal sales pitches differ? In forming your answer, think about the following questions:

- **Speak So Others Can Understand** What types of statements and questions did Omar and Leila make so that their customers understood the types of items being sold?

- **Customer Relations** How successful were Omar and Leila in applying good nonverbal communication skills to their customer interactions?

Remember!

Interact Effectively with Others Good speaking skills include knowing about your audience so you provide the right kind of information. If you are a salesperson, it is important to know the details of your products and to give the customers the most enticing details. In *Example 2*, Omar knows that many of his customers come in only to browse, so he must get them excited in order to convince them to purchase baked goods.

Try It Out! ■ ■ ■

Understanding the Audience and the Nature of Information Devon is an assistant at a library. She has been asked to give a short presentation to some three- to five-year-old children on the importance of brushing your teeth every day. Devon is used to teaching older children and is not sure that the presentation she usually uses will be appropriate for younger children. She has a colleague who works with younger children, so she calls her colleague and leaves a voice mail asking for advice. Her colleague calls her back and leaves the following voice mail.

> *Hi, Devon. I got your message, and I have some advice for you. Small children like exciting, fun presentations, so I would make sure to sound enthusiastic. They have some familiarity with toothbrushes and toothpaste, but not much more, so I would keep the information pretty basic.*

Devon has to decide whether to use her usual presentation or modify it based on her colleague's advice.

Decision-Making Process				
STEP 1: Identify the Problem	**STEP 2:** Locate, Gather, and Organize Relevant Information	**STEP 3:** Generate Alternatives	**STEP 4:** Choose a Solution	**STEP 5:** Implement the Solution
Devon needs to give a presentation to young children, but her usual presentation is suited to older children. She has to decide whether to use her usual presentation or modify it.	Devon's usual presentation is designed for older children. Devon's colleague works with younger children and has given her advice about the kind of information they respond to.	Devon can use the presentation she normally uses for older children. Devon can modify her presentation based on the advice her colleague gave her.	Devon chooses to modify her presentation based on the information her colleague gave her.	Devon changes her normal presentation to be more exciting. She also adjusts her language to use simplified vocabulary, and she cuts out some of the more advanced knowledge to keep it basic.

Devon understands that her success depends on giving a presentation that meets the needs of her specific audience. The presentation she gives is designed specifically for small children. She focuses on simple ideas, rather than complex subjects related to dental hygiene. Devon's delivery of the presentation also takes her audience into consideration. She speaks in an enthusiastic voice and frequently asks children to come up and help her model good dental hygiene skills. The children give Devon their attention and respond well to her modified presentation.

Remember!

Speak So Others Can Understand In many careers, you will need to address a wide variety of audiences. For example, you should expect to speak in a different way to your supervisor than to a family member or a friend. If you are speaking to children, you will likely need to put things more simply than you would when speaking to adults. However, if you are unsure of your audience, it is usually best to speak in a professional tone. Devon knew she needed to speak in a way that was engaging for children. It is important to speak in such a way that your audience can understand your message.

Tools for Workplace Success

Understanding the Audience and the Nature of Information Seung works as a machinist for a bottle manufacturer. His boss asks him to research a new mechanized bottle labeler to see if the new equipment might improve productivity at the factory.

> Seung gives a very detailed technical description of the machine and explains to his boss exactly how it works. He explains what types of bottles the machine is used for and how each type of bottle feeds through it and gets labeled. He even explains how the machine is assembled.

At the end of the presentation, Seung's boss seems upset. Seung asks if the presentation was helpful, and his boss tells him that it was not. His boss says that he was interested in whether the new labeler would help productivity, not a detailed description of how the machine worked.

1. Why was Seung's boss unhappy with the presentation?
   A. Seung's presentation was appropriate for any audience.
   B. Seung's presentation was overly simple and below the level of his audience.
   C. Seung gave inaccurate information in his presentation, which misled his audience.
   D. Seung's presentation did not include enough detailed information.
   E. Seung's presentation gave information that was not relevant to his audience.

2. How would Seung have changed his presentation if he had considered the needs of his audience?
   F. He would have used less technical language and focused on the overall results the machine would create.
   G. He would have made the presentation longer so it would seem more important.
   H. He would have made the presentation more complex so his boss would think he was smarter.
   J. He would have put more technical detail in the presentation so his boss would have a better idea of how the machine worked.
   K. He would have made up the information in the presentation because he did not know what his boss was looking for.

Reflect In both of the *Try It Out!* examples, Devon and Seung needed to deliver presentations for specific audiences. Devon did not have experience giving presentations to young children, so she called a colleague who had the relevant experience to ask for advice. Seung decided to give an overly technical presentation about how the new labeler worked when his boss was only interested in how it would affect productivity. In your opinion, who made the better choices in considering the needs of the audience? What consequences did their choices have? What ways could both Devon and Seung have prepared so that their presentations were appropriate for their audiences?

Remember!

Interact Effectively with Others Not all audiences are seated in an auditorium. Any time you are giving information, you have an audience. Your audience is whomever you are giving information to. You need to consider how best to approach your audience to accomplish the purpose of communicating the information. Seung's supervisor is an audience of one. Devon's group of children is another type of audience. Devon and Seung each had a different audience to approach, and each needed to choose a way of communicating that was best suited to that particular audience.

On Your Own ▪ ▪ ▪

Read the following scenarios. Then answer the questions that follow each scenario.

SCENARIO A Using Logical Organization

As the human resources coordinator for a law firm, you must explain how to enroll for health insurance benefits. You are holding a morning and an afternoon discussion.

> *Good morning. Today we are going to discuss who can enroll for health benefits. To enroll, go to the website, enter your personal information, and choose a doctor from the list of options. However, before you do that, choose what type of plan you want. You can choose either a PPO or an HMO. Remember, certain doctors aren't covered by the different plans, so you'll need to choose the plan first and then the doctor.*

The morning audience is confused about how they should enroll for benefits. You must figure out how to make the afternoon presentation less confusing.

Complete the chart below and then answer the questions that follow.

Decision-Making Process				
STEP 1: Identify the Problem	**STEP 2:** Locate, Gather, and Organize Relevant Information	**STEP 3:** Generate Alternatives	**STEP 4:** Choose a Solution	**STEP 5:** Implement the Solution
You must figure out how to make the afternoon presentation less confusing.	Your morning presentation gave the steps out of order. You need to make sure each step is presented in the right order.			

1. Why did your morning presentation cause confusion?

2. How should you change the presentation for the afternoon discussion?

SCENARIO B Recognizing and Using Nonverbal Expression

You are the manager for a hardware store. You have received some complaints about the customer service of one of your employees, so you observe his behavior.

> Your employee does not make eye contact with customers. When they enter the store, he ignores them and plays games on his cell phone.

3. What is the problem with this employee's customer service?

4. How can the employee improve his performance in the future?

SCENARIO C Using Persuasive Language

You have worked as a data entry specialist for an investment company for a year. You think that you deserve a pay raise. You make the case for a raise to your supervisor.

> *I think I deserve a raise because I show up on time, and I do good work. I've worked here for a year, so I deserve a raise.*

Your supervisor tells you that raises are based on surpassing expectations and providing measurable contributions to the company. He denies you a raise.

5. Why do you think your supervisor was not convinced by your arguments?

6. What could you have said to better persuade your manager to give you a raise?

SCENARIO D Using Common English Conventions

You are a train operator. A train in front of you is having mechanical problems and causing delays. You need to let passengers know what is happening.

> *Attention, passengers. Looks like the train up ahead is busted, so we're going to have to hang tight for a while. The maintenance crew is working on it, so we should be out of here in two shakes.*

7. What is it about your message that might confuse your passengers and why?

8. How might you phrase your message differently to be more clear?

Summary ▪ ▪ ▪

Employees who speak clearly make sure they are understood and can convey information to others. To develop good speaking skills, be sure to do the following:

- **Recognize and use nonverbal expression** Keep your arms loose at your sides and be sure to look your audience in the eye. Remember to have good posture.

- **Understand your audience** Any time you speak, you have an audience. Even if your audience is just one coworker, keep your words and tone professional.

- **Express information clearly and confidently** Make sure you have all the information you need. Knowing these details will help you speak confidently.

- **Use common English conventions** Be sure to use complete, logical sentences and appropriate word choices.

- **Use logical organization** Provide information in a logical order.

- **Use persuasive language** When you offer information in a confident tone, you will be more likely to persuade your audience.

Answers begin on page 127.

Lesson 8
Working Together

Working together means more than just showing up at the same site. You will have to acknowledge team membership and roles. Then you can form productive relationships, identify with the team and its goals, and resolve conflicts.

Skill Examples

Identifying with the Team and Its Goals Benjamin and Gary are both salespeople. They have been asked to work additional hours next week.

Read the two examples and answer the questions that follow.

EXAMPLE 1 Benjamin's Weekly Schedule

Benjamin works as a salesperson in the menswear department of a large store. The store is planning a major sale event next week. Benjamin's supervisor sends memos to all the employees notifying them of the extra hours she expects them to work. However, she does not check to find out when they are available.

MEMO

To: Benjamin
From: Susan

All employees are being asked to work extra hours next week to cover the sale event. In addition to your normal hours, you will be asked to work on Friday from 4 P.M. until 10 P.M.

Benjamin is concerned. His son has a school play on Friday evening, so he will not be able to work. He is available on Monday and Wednesday to work.

1. If Benjamin refuses to work the extra hours, what consequences might he face?
   A. His supervisor might commend him for standing up for himself.
   B. He might be reprimanded for not following his supervisor's directions.
   C. His supervisor might be pleased to offer the hours to someone else.
   D. His son might be disappointed that his father cannot attend the play.
   E. His coworkers might be happy that nobody has to work on Friday.

2. How could Benjamin's supervisor have worked with the team to better prepare for the sale?
   F. She could have required all employees to work all the extra hours instead of splitting the extra hours between them.
   G. She could have asked only the best employees to work extra hours.
   H. She could have refused to ask her employees to work extra hours.
   J. She could have asked employees when they would be available to work extra hours.
   K. She could have decided to work all the extra hours herself.

Remember!

Communication and Collaboration Do not assume people know what is happening in your life outside of work. In *Example 1,* Benjamin's supervisor could have made an effort to ask Benjamin about his Friday availability. Benjamin could also have made sure to tell his supervisor about his son's play so she would know that this is an important event Benjamin cannot miss. He could also communicate his concerns to his supervisor after he receives the memo. She might understand and revise the schedule. Alternatively, Benjamin could ask a coworker to switch shifts with him and ask his supervisor to approve it. It is important to offer solutions when presented with a problem like this.

EXAMPLE 2 Gary's Weekly Schedule

Gary works in the furniture department of the same store as Benjamin. His supervisor has also been asked to schedule extra employees for the sale. Before the sale-week schedule is posted, Gary's supervisor posts the following memo.

> ## MEMO
>
> **To:** Furniture Department Staff
> **From:** Sandra Escobar, Sales Manager
>
> Due to the sales event later this month, everyone is required to work extra hours. I hope we can all work together to meet the company's goals. Please notify me which hours next week you are available to work. I will do my best to accommodate everyone's schedule, but conflicts may prevent me from meeting everyone's needs.

Gary responds that he has a dentist appointment on Tuesday morning. He is not available then, but he is available on all other days. When the schedule is posted, Gary is off on Tuesday morning.

3. Based on her actions, how does Gary's supervisor show that she identifies with her team and their goals?

   A. She requests that all her employees work both Monday and Tuesday during the sales rush.

   B. She offers her team an opportunity to balance personal and professional obligations.

   C. She decides on her own which extra hours each employee will work.

   D. She lets Gary make the schedule for everyone's extra hours this week.

   E. She never allows employees to switch shifts after the schedule is posted.

4. If Gary had been asked to work Tuesday morning, what could he do to effectively resolve the problem?

   F. He could refuse to show up for work on Tuesday.

   G. He could request to work in a different department on Tuesday.

   H. He could request to switch shifts with another employee for Tuesday.

   J. He could tell his supervisor that the extra hours requirement is unfair.

   K. He could go to the dentist and hope the appointment is short enough for him to still get to work.

Think About It Both Benjamin's and Gary's supervisors were given the task of scheduling their employees for extra hours. However, each supervisor handled it differently. Which supervisor's approach was more effective? In forming your answer, think about the following questions:

- **Cooperate with Others** What do the actions of the two supervisors show about their willingness to cooperate with others to meet common goals?

- **Manage Goals and Time** How successful was each supervisor in managing her employees' time? Explain.

Remember!

Be Flexible Sometimes, you will be asked to go above and beyond your typical job requirements in order to help your team achieve a goal. Try to be flexible in these situations, and you may find that others are more flexible with you when you are in need of a favor. In *Example 2*, Gary is willing to work the extra hours, and he communicates the hours he is available to his supervisor ahead of time to try to avoid a conflict.

Try It Out! ■ ■ ■

Resolving Conflicts Gerard is a teller at a local bank. The bank's managers have decided to donate some money to a local cause. They have asked the bank tellers to choose which local cause they should support.

E-mail Message
To: Hamlet Hills Bank Tellers
Subject: Local Cause
As some of you may already know, management has asked our tellers to choose a local cause that we as a bank would like to support financially. Please work together to come to a group solution. We are excited about this opportunity to support the local community and hope that you are too. Best wishes, Darien Johnson Financial Manager

Gerard's daughter is on a Little League baseball team that is currently searching for a sponsor. Gerard suggests this cause to the group, but there are two other local causes that his coworkers have suggested, and the group's support is divided among the three different causes. Management wants to support only one cause, so the group must figure out how to agree on the one to choose.

Decision-Making Process

STEP 1: Identify the Problem	STEP 2: Locate, Gather, and Organize Relevant Information	STEP 3: Generate Alternatives	STEP 4: Choose a Solution	STEP 5: Implement the Solution
Gerard and his coworkers need to choose one cause to support, and Gerard hopes they choose his daughter's team.	Other tellers also have nominated causes that are personally meaningful to them. The bank will support only one local cause.	Gerard can demand that the tellers help his daughter's team. Gerard can suggest that the tellers have a secret vote on all the nominated causes.	He chooses to propose that the tellers hold a secret ballot to vote on all the nominated causes.	Gerard asks a bank manager to read the secret ballots to make sure everyone followed the voting rules. One cause is the clear winner.

Gerard realizes that not everyone feels the same way about his daughter's team as he does, no progress is being made, and something needs to change. He decides that the best way to get the group to come to an agreement is to take a secret vote, so he proposes this idea to the rest of the group. They agree, and a vote is held. The cause that gets the most votes is a local soup kitchen that provides food and shelter to homeless veterans. Gerard is a bit disappointed, but he feels that the decision was fair.

Establishing Productive Relationships Aisha works as a copy editor for a local news agency. She is also the chairperson of a ten-member committee that is trying to decide how to use profits from the previous year. Seven of the committee members want to reinvest the money into the news agency by purchasing better-quality video cameras. The other three members think the profits should be divided among the agency employees as year-end bonuses. Rather than discuss the point any further or try to reach a compromise, Aisha decides to go with the majority opinion. She sends the following e-mail to everyone in the agency.

E-mail Message

To: All Employees

Subject: Profit Reallocation Committee

After much consideration, all members of the Profits Allocation Committee are pleased to announce our agreed-upon decision. Profits from the previous fiscal year will be reinvested into the agency by purchasing better-quality video cameras.

When the three committee members who supported year-end bonuses receive the e-mail, they are very upset. They did not agree to the final decision and are angry that the e-mail claims that "all members" of the committee are in agreement. They decide to speak to Aisha about their concerns.

1. How might Aisha's actions affect her coworkers' views of her?
   A. They might see her as someone who is willing to compromise.
   B. They might see her as someone who values compromise over bonuses.
   C. They might see her as someone who is unwilling to compromise.
   D. They might see her as someone who values teamwork over compromise.
   E. They might see her as the only person on the committee who values compromise.

2. How might Aisha's relationships with the three committee members have been different if she had scheduled another meeting to reach a compromise?
   F. They would have respected Aisha's attempt to reach a compromise.
   G. They would have been frustrated that Aisha did not agree with their opinion.
   H. They would have thought that Aisha did not value their opinions.
   J. They would have been relieved that Aisha agreed with them about giving out bonuses.
   K. They would have been angry that Aisha is wasting their time with another meeting.

Reflect In each of the *Try It Out!* examples, Aisha and Gerard had to decide how to reach an agreement in a group with divided opinions. In which of the scenarios do you think the decision was fair? In what ways can both Aisha and Gerard exhibit good teamwork skills once a final decision is reached?

Remember!

Sociability Sometimes when you work with a team, you will have a different opinion than other members of your team. If you have very good reasons for feeling differently, be prepared to speak up and support your opinion with facts. If the group cannot reach an agreement, sometimes you have to take a vote. Aisha decided in favor of the opinion of the majority of the group without holding a discussion or taking a vote. This led the minority to feel like they were not being treated fairly. Allowing for discussion of differing opinions and holding a vote are good ways to reach an agreement. These processes help team members feel that their voices are heard and valued and help foster productive relationships.

On Your Own ▪ ■ ■

Read the following scenarios. Then answer the questions that follow each scenario.

SCENARIO A Establishing Productive Relationships

You are an elementary school teacher. You have a teaching assistant, Heather, who is in college. You want to reorganize the classroom, and you ask for Heather's opinion. She offers some suggestions, but you organize the classroom in a different way.

> Heather comes into the classroom the morning after you reorganize it. She is upset. She approaches you and wants to know why you did not take her opinions seriously. You felt that Heather's ideas were interesting. However, based on your experience, you knew they were not practical. Heather is a good teacher's assistant, and you do not want to discourage her enthusiasm.

Complete the chart below and then answer the questions that follow.

Decision-Making Process				
STEP 1: Identify the Problem	**STEP 2:** Locate, Gather, and Organize Relevant Information	**STEP 3:** Generate Alternatives	**STEP 4:** Choose a Solution	**STEP 5:** Implement the Solution
You did not implement Heather's suggestions, and now she thinks you do not value her opinions.	You thought Heather's ideas were innovative. You did not think her ideas were practical.			

1. In what way can you make Heather feel like a valued member of the team?

2. If Heather feels valued, how will this affect both you and the children in your classroom?

SCENARIO B Identifying with the Team and Its Goals

As the foreman of a landscaping crew, your job includes assigning tasks to your crew.

> You tend to give the most physically demanding jobs to other people. You work long days since your role as a foreman includes completing paperwork as well as the physical work of landscaping. Your crew often complains that they are required to do all the hard work while you stay in your truck doing paperwork.

3. What is the main conflict between you and your crew?

4. What solutions can you think of to improve your relationship with your crew and their impression of you?

5. What consequences might these solutions have?

SCENARIO C Acknowledging Team Membership and Role

As an advertising manager for a pet grooming company, you are the leader of a small team that is trying to come up with ideas for a television commercial. In the morning, you schedule a meeting for that afternoon but forget to describe its purpose.

> You begin the first group meeting by outlining a few of your ideas for the commercial. When you ask the team to share their ideas, nobody speaks up. When you ask them to comment on your ideas, they do not offer any feedback. One member says he does not know anything about commercials.

6. What problem is preventing your team from working together on the commercial?

7. What directions can you give the group to help them prepare for the next meeting?

SCENARIO D Resolving Conflicts

You work as an accountant for a publishing company. Your supervisor mentions that she has noticed you tend to submit your reports at the last minute.

> Your reports depend on information that is supplied by a dozen different salespeople. Some salespeople are frequently late in submitting their reports to you. When they submit late reports, you get stuck working late hours in order to get your reports in on time. You are upset that your supervisor is critical of you. You feel that you are doing everything you can to submit your reports on time.

8. What is the problem you must solve in this scenario?

9. What solutions can you implement to get the salespeople to submit their reports in a more timely manner?

Summary ▪ ▪ ▪

When you and others are working together to achieve a common goal, conflicts are inevitable. To start developing good teamwork skills, be sure to do the following:

- **Acknowledge team membership and roles** If you are the team leader, guide your team by collecting relevant information and getting organized. If you are a team member, do your best to support the team leader by offering suggestions.

- **Establish productive relationships** Avoid seeing team members or team leaders as competition. Instead, respect and value their ideas and contributions.

- **Identify with the team and its goals** If you are assigned to a new team, ask questions to find out the most important goals of the team.

- **Resolve conflicts** It is okay for people to disagree—what is more important is that you and your team members work together to develop solutions.

Answers begin on page 128.

Managing Yourself ...

To be an effective employee, you do not have to change your personality, but you do have to practice self-control and other self-management skills. Employers expect employees to remain responsible, calm, and professional in even the most difficult situations.

In Theme 3, you will learn about important self-management skills.

Lesson 9: Being an Ethical Employee Respectful, fair, and honest employees work well with others and encourage their peers to behave in the same way.
Objectives include:

- Abiding By a Strict Code of Ethics and Behavior
- Making Objective Decisions
- Encouraging Others to Act Ethically
- Treating Others with Honesty, Fairness, and Respect
- Abiding By a Strict Ethical Code

Lesson 10: Being Responsible Responsible behavior in the workplace requires accountability, efficiency, and the ability to learn from mistakes.
Objectives include:

- Demonstrating a Willingness to Work
- Taking Responsibility for Actions
- Accomplishing Work Goals Within Accepted Time Frames
- Learning from Mistakes

Lesson 11: Managing Your Time Employees who manage their time can plan ahead, complete tasks efficiently, and overcome obstacles in order to meet deadlines. *Objectives include*:

- Prioritizing
- Allocating Resources
- Planning
- Anticipating Obstacles

Lesson 12: Being Professional Maintaining self-control and a positive attitude are vital skills to master in the workplace. *Objectives include*:

- Demonstrating Self-Control
- Maintaining a Professional Appearance
- Balancing Work and Life
- Maintaining a Positive Attitude

Key Factors for Managing Yourself ▪ ▪ ▪

These lessons will help you identify and practice behaviors necessary for self-management. Employers value employees who can manage themselves because these employees are responsible, motivated, and independent. To effectively and consistently manage yourself in the workplace, you must be able to:

- **Be responsible** Responsible employees fulfill their obligations and complete their tasks. Demonstrating responsibility shows employers that you are trustworthy.

- **Demonstrate integrity** Integrity is one of the most important characteristics employers look for in potential candidates. Employees who are able to make good decisions and demonstrate honesty are of great value to a company.

- **Monitor and correct performance** Monitoring the quality of work is necessary for fulfilling company expectations. Employees who are able to identify areas for improvement, learn from mistakes, and continuously improve their performance are able to thrive and advance in their positions.

Knowing how to manage yourself will make you more effective in the workplace. It will also help you gain the respect of both employers and coworkers.

Remember!
Managing yourself is a skill that can benefit you, your coworkers, and others in your personal and professional life. Taking responsibility, practicing ethical behaviors, prioritizing, and other self-management skills will show employers that you are serious and professional.

Lesson 9 ▪ ▪ ▪
Being an Ethical Employee

Behaving ethically and fairly is important in any profession. Fair and ethical employees abide by a strict code of behavior and encourage others to do the same. They also make objective decisions and treat others with honesty, fairness, and respect.

Skill Examples ▪ ▪ ▪

Abiding By a Strict Ethical Code Daniela and Mark both work in professions that require them to interact with diverse people. They do not always get along with the people they work with.

Read the two examples and answer the questions that follow.

EXAMPLE 1 **Daniela's Decision**

> Daniela is an administrative assistant for a lobbying firm. She enjoys her job and likes her coworkers. Michael and Lin are two of the senior lobbyists whom Daniela works with. Daniela finds Michael much easier to get along with than Lin. She makes a special effort to organize Michael's files and always reserves the best conference room for his clients. Today, Lin asks Daniela to copy an urgent file. Daniela decides that it can wait until she has scheduled rooms for Michael's meetings tomorrow.

1. What might happen as a result of Daniela waiting to copy the file for Lin?
   A. Lin might be happy that Michael's meetings have been scheduled.
   B. Lin might begin treating Daniela better.
   C. Lin might not be able to complete her work on time.
   D. Lin might not let Daniela work with Michael anymore.
   E. Lin might begin to compete with Michael for Daniela's time and attention.

2. What would have happened if Daniela had not let her personal feelings about Lin and Michael influence her work?
   F. She would have showed that she could prioritize and treat others fairly.
   G. She would have proved that she could do multiple tasks at once.
   H. She would have showed that she was able to meet urgent deadlines.
   J. She would have earned a reputation as an employee who picks favorites.
   K. She would have been able to get all her tasks done by the end of the day.

Remember!

Work with Others

When you make decisions in the workplace, try to keep your personal feelings out of the process. Treat all coworkers equally and prioritize tasks according to their importance, rather than your feelings about your coworkers. In *Example 1*, Daniela chooses to complete a low-priority task for a colleague with whom she is friendly before a high-priority task for a colleague she does not personally like. By rearranging her tasks, she can show that she is a fair and ethical employee.

EXAMPLE 2 Mark's Observation

Mark is a meat packer at a processing plant. When he started the job, he learned the importance of practicing good hygiene at work. Mark always makes sure he washes his hands before his shift and every time he goes to the bathroom. However, he notices that his coworker Kai has not been following the same example. Mark lives near Kai, and they have been friends for a long time. Mark decides to casually mention the issue to him. When Kai refuses to wash his hands after the third reminder, Mark reports him to their supervisor.

3. Based on Mark's actions, how might his supervisor perceive him?

A. as a fair and ethical employee

B. as a sneaky employee who causes trouble for others

C. as a poorly skilled employee who cannot perform his job

D. as a nosy employee who pays too much attention to what other people are doing

E. as a punctual and efficient employee

4. What might have happened if Mark had decided not to report his friend's behavior?

F. Mark might have been promoted faster.

G. Mark might have risked the health of the company's customers.

H. Mark might have been disciplined for discrimination.

J. Mark might have been moved to a different processing role.

K. Mark might have been fined for his poor hygiene.

Think About It Think about Daniela's and Mark's actions. How did each of them balance their personal feelings with their work responsibilities? How does this balance reflect their ethical behavior? In forming your answer, think about the following questions:

- **Work with Others** How did Daniela and Mark work with others, and how did their attitudes toward others affect their workplace decisions?

- **Integrity** Did Daniela and Mark display integrity? Why or why not?

Remember!

Responsibility
Sometimes personal relationships in the workplace may conflict with your ethical responsibilities. In *Example 2*, Mark ensures that his close relationship with Kai does not interfere with his responsibility to report a health code violation. He understands that the possible consequences of breaking the rules are more important than his personal feelings.

Try It Out! ■ ■ ■

Making Objective Decisions Juanita is a meeting planner for an educational research institution. She is in charge of finding a location for an upcoming conference. She has narrowed down the choices to two possible venues. While she is deciding which would better suit the organization's needs, she receives the following voice mail from the manager at one of the venues.

> *Hi, Ms. Gonzalez, this is Christine from the Inspire Hotel Group. I just wanted to check in with you to see whether you've made a decision about holding the Spring Forum here in April. I also wanted to let you know that we can offer you and one other guest three free nights at the hotel. We'll also throw in one of our luxury spa packages. Call me at (301) 555–0172 when you've made your decision.*

Juanita has not had a vacation in a long time and is impressed by the hotel's luxury facilities. However, the other venue has a larger conference room and is slightly cheaper. She does not know what to do.

Remember!

Decision Making

Sometimes you may not be sure whether a decision is ethical. In these cases, consider how you would feel if your clients and coworkers knew the factors that led to your decision. Juanita's supervisor may have been upset if he knew Juanita accepted a gift from one of the hotels since this might have influenced her decision.

Decision-Making Process				
STEP 1: Identify the Problem	**STEP 2:** Locate, Gather, and Organize Relevant Information	**STEP 3:** Generate Alternatives	**STEP 4:** Choose a Solution	**STEP 5:** Implement the Solution
Juanita is choosing between two hotels for a conference, and one of the hotels has offered her a free stay and spa package.	One venue has a larger conference room and is slightly cheaper. Although the other venue is smaller and costs more, it is suitable. The venue has also offered Juanita three nights free.	Juanita can accept the offer for the free stay and take advantage of the gift. Juanita can decline the offer for the free stay and book the conference at the hotel with the larger conference room.	Juanita does not want to be enticed by the free stay. She also knows that the first venue will better suit her organization's needs. She chooses the hotel with the larger conference room that is slightly cheaper.	Juanita refuses the offer of the free stay from the hotel and books the forum at the other venue with the larger conference room.

Juanita must choose between two venues for her organization's Spring Forum. Both are acceptable choices. However, one has a larger conference room. The other has a smaller conference room but offered Juanita a free stay. Juanita is tempted by the offer of a free stay, but she knows that she has to make an objective decision based on what is best for her company. She decides to turn down the free stay and spa package so she can remain objective. She books the venue with the larger conference room since it is better for her company. By doing so, Juanita shows that she is able to make an unbiased decision.

Encouraging Others to Act Ethically Caleb is a cashier in a department store cafeteria. During his regular weekday shift, he chats with Rahul, who is also a cashier at the cafeteria.

> *RAHUL: I could barely afford to pay my rent this week.*
> *CALEB: Tell me about it, I've been eating instant noodles all month. We could really do with a raise.*
> *RAHUL: Hey, I think that customer just accidentally gave me an extra $20. It was stuck to the other bill. Man, that would really help with this week's groceries.*
> *CALEB: Yeah, but imagine how you'd feel if you lost $20.*
> *RAHUL: I'm imagining how I feel about having an extra $20 for groceries! Do you think he'll notice he lost the bill?*
> *CALEB: That doesn't matter. Even if we eat instant noodles, we can get by. We shouldn't take someone else's money.*
> *RAHUL: Yeah, I guess you're right.*
> *CALEB: I can see the guy over by the silverware. You should go and give the twenty back to him.*

After a moment's hesitation, Rahul leaves his cash register and returns the money to the customer.

1. How did Caleb's actions influence Rahul?
   A. Caleb convinced Rahul that they did not need a raise.
   B. Caleb convinced Rahul to keep the $20 bill.
   C. Caleb convinced Rahul to wait to see if the man noticed the money was missing before returning it.
   D. Caleb convinced Rahul that the fair thing to do was to return the money.
   E. Caleb convinced Rahul that it was fair to use the money to pay for Rahul's groceries.

2. What might have happened if Caleb had remained silent when Rahul mentioned keeping the money?
   F. Rahul might not have had enough money for groceries that week.
   G. Caleb might have been punished and fired for keeping the money.
   H. Caleb might have avoided being fired because he had not participated.
   J. Caleb and Rahul might have been promoted and given a pay rise.
   K. Caleb and Rahul might have been disciplined or even fired for their actions.

Reflect In both of the *Try It Out!* examples, the employees made decisions about whether to behave fairly and ethically in their workplaces. Do you think they made the correct decisions? What factors did they consider when making their decisions? Were these the most important factors to consider? How might the outcomes of the situations have changed if they had considered different factors?

Remember!

Integrity Part of being a fair and ethical employee is treating others the way you want to be treated. Caleb imagined how he would have felt if a cashier had been dishonest with him. He would have been upset and wished the cashier had been honest. If you are having trouble figuring out the right course of action, think about how the other person might feel. This should make it easier to make the correct decision.

On Your Own ■ ■ ■

Read the following scenarios. Then answer the questions that follow each scenario.

SCENARIO A Treating Others with Honesty, Fairness, and Respect

You are a carpenter for an off-Broadway show. As one of the set builders, you report directly to the master carpenter.

The opening night for the production is approaching, and stress levels are high. You misinterpret one of the master carpenter's directions and build a square table instead of a round one. The master carpenter blames one of the junior stagehands for your mistake and shouts at her in front of the rest of the crew. You know it was not the stagehand's fault, but you do not want to get in trouble with the master carpenter.

Complete the chart below and then answer the questions that follow.

Decision-Making Process				
STEP 1: Identify the Problem	**STEP 2:** Locate, Gather, and Organize Relevant Information	**STEP 3:** Generate Alternatives	**STEP 4:** Choose a Solution	**STEP 5:** Implement the Solution
You made a mistake, and someone else is being blamed for it. You are unsure whether to admit that the error was your fault.	You built a table in the wrong shape, wasting precious resources. A colleague is being blamed for your mistake.			

1. What are some alternative ways to solve this problem?

2. What are all the possible consequences for the solutions you generated?

SCENARIO B Abiding By a Strict Code of Ethics and Behavior

You are an accounting assistant. You recently left your job at Thomson & Thomson to work at a rival company.

Your new supervisor tells you that one of your first projects will be to help her pursue new clients in the travel industry. In essence, the project requires you to try to steal clients away from established companies. Your supervisor asks you to send her a list of your old company's major clients (with pay rates if possible). This will help her get a head start on the project.

3. What is the problem with this situation?

4. What solution would you choose to resolve this situation?

5. Who would you communicate with regarding your solution?

SCENARIO C Making Objective Decisions

You work as a childcare development specialist at an after-school program. The program has a long waiting list. You receive the following voice mail.

> *Hey, it's Krista and Neil here. Listen, we've been trying to get Nisha into your after-school program and it's totally full. We had no idea there was such a long waiting list. I know it's a lot to ask, but is there any way you can put in a good word for us at the next intake? We'd really like to get her in as soon as possible; she's a little behind on her reading. Give us a call when you can. Thanks!*

You want to help your friends, but your after-school program requires that parents follow a proper enrollment process. You are unsure of what to do.

6. What are some alternative solutions that you can take to resolve this situation?

7. What are the positive and negative consequences for each solution that you listed?

SCENARIO D Encouraging Others to Act Ethically

You are a roofer who works for a construction company that has multiple job sites. When you finish your tasks, you are expected to see if you are needed at other sites.

> You and your team must complete the scaffolding on the roof of an apartment block. It is close to the end of the day, and you have finished the task. Your coworkers want to leave and not check in. You point out that you have often needed help and it would be wrong to abandon other teams that might need it.

8. What information do you have available about this problem?

9. What solution would you choose to implement?

Summary ▪ ▪ ▪

Employees who are fair and ethical make decisions based on objective criteria. To ensure that you are a fair and ethical employee, be sure to do the following:

- **Abide by a strict code of ethics and behavior** Keep confidential information to yourself and follow company regulations.

- **Encourage others to act ethically** Provide a positive example for others to follow, and encourage them to behave fairly and ethically.

- **Treat others with honesty, fairness, and respect** Treat people equally and as you would like to be treated, no matter your feelings or the people's behaviors.

- **Make objective decisions** Make decisions based on the best interests of your customers, clients, and company, rather than personal gain.

Answers begin on page 129.

Lesson 10
Being Responsible

Personal responsibility is important in all aspects of life, but it is extremely important in the workplace. Responsible workers own their actions and learn from their mistakes. They complete assigned tasks efficiently and are also willing to do additional work if needed.

Skill Examples

Taking Responsibility for Actions Mei and Gunther both work in the customer service industry. They often have to deal with unsatisfied customers.

Read the two examples and answer the questions that follow.

EXAMPLE 1 Mei's Customer Service

Mei works as a food preparation worker at a local deli. During the lunch rush, a customer orders a chicken salad sandwich on wheat bread with no dressing. Mei makes the sandwich but accidentally adds ranch dressing. She makes the customer a totally new sandwich. When Mei hands the customer his sandwich, he makes a rude comment about the length of time it took to make. Mei tells the customer that she is not sure what he is talking about and that he did not have to wait too long for his sandwich.

1. Based on Mei's actions, why might her manager perceive that she does not take responsibility?
   A. She refuses to admit that she made a mistake.
   B. She does not know how to make a chicken salad sandwich.
   C. She is not willing to make the customer another sandwich.
   D. She is not supposed to talk to the customer.
   E. She does not practice good hygiene when she prepares food.

2. What might have happened if Mei had admitted her mistake and apologized to the customer for taking too long?
   F. She might have been fired from her job.
   G. She might have showed that she is able to take responsibility.
   H. She might have angered the customer further.
   J. She might have had to remake the customer's sandwich again.
   K. She might have been forced to pay for the customer's sandwich.

Remember!

Customer Relations In reality, the customer is not always right. Customers can be rude or demanding. However, even when customers are incorrect, it is important to remain polite and professional. In *Example 1,* the customer made a rude comment toward Mei. Instead of getting upset, Mei should have maintained a professional manner and calmly explained the reason for the delay.

EXAMPLE 2 Gunther's Customer Service

Gunther is an electrician for a small company. He is tasked with installing a complex electrical wiring system in a new extension of a client's house. After he completes the job, he heads back to the office to gather his personal belongings and go home for the day. When he gets to the office, he finds out that the owner of the house called to complain that the power is out in the basement. Gunther calls the customer and apologizes for the problem. He promises to go back early the following morning. The next day, Gunther returns to the house and fixes the problem.

3. How do Gunther's actions show that he takes responsibility for his work?

   A. He installs a complex electrical wiring system.

   B. He returns to the office after finishing his job.

   C. He admits to his mistake and corrects the problem as soon as possible.

   D. He cuts the power in the homeowner's basement.

   E. He does not immediately return to the house to fix the problem.

4. What might have happened if Gunther had not admitted his mistake?

   F. The homeowner might have given the company a good review.

   G. The homeowner might have viewed Gunther as irresponsible and unprofessional.

   H. Gunther's manager might have praised him for his actions.

   J. Gunther might have shown that he was responsible and willing to learn from his mistakes.

   K. Gunther's manager might have decided to give Gunther easier jobs to work on in the future.

Think About It Think about how Mei and Gunther dealt with their customers. Which one of them is more likely to be evaluated positively? In forming your answer, think about the following questions:

- **Decision Making** How might Mei's and Gunther's actions influence their supervisors' opinion of them? What might the consequences be for them? How might their actions affect their companies?

- **Monitor and Correct Performance** What might have happened if Mei and Gunther had acted differently? How might Gunther's relationship with his customer be affected if he had refused to admit his mistake or had taken longer to resolve the problem?

Remember!

Monitor and Correct Performance No matter what your career or position, you are bound to make mistakes. Accept that this will happen, and make an effort to learn from your errors. After his experience in *Example 2*, Gunther knows that for future jobs he should check the power in other areas of the house before leaving the job site. Treating errors as a learning opportunity will help you improve your performance and avoid similar mistakes in the future.

Try It Out! ▪ ■ ■

Taking Responsibility for Actions Sunil works for a large corporation as an audio-visual technician. He regularly sets up recording equipment for important meetings so that company executives have a record of any decisions that were made.

> Sunil's boss asks him to record a very important meeting involving new clients. Sunil has just finished setting up the recording equipment when his phone rings. It is a coworker with an urgent question. Sunil leaves the conference room to answer his coworker's query. When he returns, the meeting has already started. Sunil does not manage to record the first ten minutes.

Sunil knows that he should have recorded the entire meeting. He does not think that he missed anything important, but he cannot be sure.

Decision-Making Process				
STEP 1: Identify the Problem	**STEP 2:** Locate, Gather, and Organize Relevant Information	**STEP 3:** Generate Alternatives	**STEP 4:** Choose a Solution	**STEP 5:** Implement the Solution
Sunil fails to record the first ten minutes of an important meeting.	Sunil takes a call from a coworker and misses the first ten minutes of the meeting. Sunil does not know if he missed anything important.	Sunil can give his boss a copy of the recording and hope that no one notices it does not start at the beginning of the meeting. Sunil can explain the situation to his boss and apologize for his mistake.	Sunil does not think that he missed anything important, but he does not want to cause any future problems for the company. He chooses to tell his boss what happened.	Sunil asks to speak with his boss, explains the situation, and apologizes for his error.

Sunil records all but the first ten minutes of the meeting. He does not think that he missed anything important, but he is not sure. His first option is to give his boss a copy of the recording and hope no one notices that it does not start at the beginning of the meeting. However, he knows that this might cause problems for his company later on. Sunil decides to take responsibility for his actions and let his boss know the situation. Acting responsibly and quickly can make a difference. Sunil's boss is able to inform those at the meeting that the first ten minutes were not recorded and ask them to share information while they are likely to remember it.

Remember!

Self-Management Do not allow other people or personal business to distract you. For example, if you receive a personal call, allow it to go to voice mail. Answer all business calls and prioritize tasks based on the caller's needs and the importance of the request. Focus on the top priority first. If Sunil had done this, he would have been able to tape the entire meeting.

Demonstrating a Willingness to Work Miles is an employee benefits representative for a sales company. He usually answers employees' queries about benefits and compensation policies, or works with insurance providers to negotiate better terms and benefits. On Tuesday morning, he arrives at the office to find the following voice mail from his boss.

> *Hi Miles, this is Terry. Listen, a couple of people in the accounting department have called in sick today. They're pretty swamped, and I was wondering if you'd mind helping out. It's nothing too taxing, mostly filing and proofing spreadsheets. Swing by my office when you get in today and we'll discuss the details. Thanks, Miles!*

Miles does not have any accounting experience and has tasks of his own to complete. However, none of his projects is urgent, which will allow him to help out elsewhere. He knocks on his boss's door and tells him that he would be happy to help out in the accounting department for the day.

1. How might Miles's decision affect his boss's opinion of him?
   A. His boss will likely view him as a flexible and willing employee.
   B. His boss will likely view him as a lazy employee who is trying to avoid doing his work.
   C. His boss will likely view him as a struggling employee who needs more training.
   D. His boss will likely view him as better suited to the accounting department.
   E. His boss will likely view him as a healthy employee who does not get sick often.

2. What might have happened if Miles had refused to help out the accounting department?
   F. He might have been given the day off from work.
   G. His boss might have signed him up for an accounting course.
   H. His coworkers in the human resources department might have been overworked.
   J. He might have given the impression that he is difficult and inflexible.
   K. He might have been assigned twice as much work as usual in his own department.

Reflect In both of the *Try It Out!* examples, the employees made decisions about taking responsibility in the workplace. Do you think they made the correct decisions? What did their decisions reveal about their attitudes in the workplace? How might the outcomes of the situations have changed if the employees had held different attitudes and made different decisions?

Remember!

Responsibility Being part of a workplace is similar to being part of a team. Sometimes you will need to help out a team member by performing tasks above or below your normal responsibilities. In the example, Miles is asked to help out on tasks outside of his department that he does not normally do, such as proofing spreadsheets. If you complete tasks like this without complaint, you demonstrate that you are willing to work as part of a team.

On Your Own ▪ ▪ ▪

Read the following scenarios. Then answer the questions that follow each scenario.

SCENARIO A Accomplishing Work Goals within Accepted Time Frames

You are a salesperson at a local clothing boutique. One of your main responsibilities is to assist customers in the dressing rooms.

> A customer in a dressing room asks you to bring her the dress that she likes in a smaller size. On your way to the rack to exchange it, another customer stops you to ask a question. You are distracted and completely forget about the customer in the dressing room. By the time you have finished helping the second customer, at least ten minutes have passed. You are unsure whether the first customer is still waiting or has given up and left the store.

Complete the chart below and then answer the questions that follow.

Decision-Making Process				
STEP 1: Identify the Problem	**STEP 2:** Locate, Gather, and Organize Relevant Information	**STEP 3:** Generate Alternatives	**STEP 4:** Choose a Solution	**STEP 5:** Implement the Solution
You are in the middle of helping a customer when you get distracted and forget about her.	At least ten minutes have passed since you left the dressing room. You are unsure whether she is still waiting.			

1. What are some alternative ways to solve this problem?

2. What solution did you choose to solve this problem? How might your solution help you learn how to deal with future mistakes?

SCENARIO B Learning from Mistakes

As a dry cleaner, you need to pay careful attention to the type of fabric that is being cleaned. Each fabric requires a specific cleaning product.

> Yesterday, you misread the label on a suit and applied bleaching powder to a stain when you should have used a gentler cleaning product. The stain became even more noticeable, and there was nothing you could do to remove it. The customer and your supervisor were very unhappy about the mistake. Today, you receive suits with similar stains. You do not know what to do. You want to use the bleaching powder, but you remember what happened yesterday.

3. How would you proceed?

4. What are the consequences of the solution you chose in Question 3?

SCENARIO C Taking Responsibility for Actions

You are a landscaper. Your business depends on word-of-mouth recommendations.

> One of your tasks is to replant seeds and bulbs. One of your clients calls to tell you that a shrub you planted last year does not look healthy. It should have come into bloom by now, but it is still bare. The next day, you dig up the shrub and replant a sapling. Later on, you realize that you have planted the wrong type of bush. The customer originally had a low-growing shrub with a blue flower. She now has a red flowering plant that will grow at least three feet tall.

5. What are some alternative solutions that you could take to resolve this situation?

6. Which solution would you choose? Why would you choose it?

SCENARIO D Demonstrating a Willingness to Work

You have recently been hired as a security guard for a shopping mall. You are eager to get started and show that you are a valuable employee. On Friday afternoon, your supervisor calls the entire security team into her office for a brief meeting.

> *Next weekend, we have a very special event taking place at the mall. Teen pop sensation Christina Rouseau has agreed to perform her new single right here. We'll need extra security to deal with the extra crowds and make sure we don't have any trouble. I'll need volunteers. Who's going to help me out?*

You have plans to hang out with friends next weekend. You are not sure what to do.

7. What are some alternative solutions to this problem? What are the pros and cons of each solution?

8. Which solution would you choose to implement?

Summary ▪ ▪ ▪

Employees who take responsibility for their actions admit to and learn from their mistakes. To ensure that you are responsible, be sure to do the following:

- **Accomplish work goals within accepted time frames** Complete tasks within the deadline that you are given.

- **Demonstrate a willingness to work** Be willing to take on additional responsibilities outside your job description and work additional hours if needed.

- **Take responsibility for actions** Admit when you make a mistake, inform the relevant person about your error, and offer to correct it.

- **Learn from mistakes** Learn from your errors so you do not make the same mistake twice.

Answers begin on page 130.

Lesson 11 ■ ■ ■
Managing Your Time

Managing time effectively is an important part of any career or position. Employees who effectively manage their time plan ahead and prioritize their tasks. They also allocate resources and anticipate obstacles that might get in the way of completing a job.

Skill Examples ■ ■ ■

Prioritizing Marisol and Golda both work in professions that require them to work on several different tasks at the same time. They find that some days are much busier than others.

Read the two examples and answer the questions that follow.

EXAMPLE 1 Marisol's Cataloging Task

Marisol works as a library assistant. On Monday morning, the head librarian asks her to catalog three boxes of archived magazines by the end of the day. Marisol finds that Mondays are one of the busiest days of the week. She has to inspect and replace all the books that were left in the drop box over the weekend. She also has to put plastic covers on all the new books that have been delivered and enter them into the computer system. Marisol works on all three tasks throughout the day. By closing time, she has not managed to finish cataloging the magazines.

1. What might the consequences of Marisol's actions be?
   A. The librarian will be pleased with Marisol.
   B. Library patrons will be charged for overdue books.
   C. The librarian may think that Marisol should not work on Mondays.
   D. The librarian may think that Marisol is good at sharing her workload.
   E. Library patrons may not be able to find the resources they need.

2. What would probably have happened if Marisol had prioritized her tasks and worked on the archiving project first?
   F. She would have gotten in trouble for not emptying the drop box.
   G. She would not have had time to finish the archiving project.
   H. She would have completed the archiving project on time.
   J. She would have been asked to stay late to complete the rest of the tasks.
   K. She would have showed that she was able to allocate resources.

Remember!

Self-Management

Sometimes you may not be able to meet your deadlines. If after you prioritize your tasks, it still seems that you will not meet your deadlines, it is important to be proactive. Notify your supervisor, ask others for help, or offer an alternative solution. In *Example 1*, Marisol should have prioritized her tasks. Then, if necessary, she could have notified her supervisor and asked for help.

Tools for Workplace Success

EXAMPLE 2 Golda's Documenting Task

Golda is a lab technician for a pharmaceutical company. The company is in the process of testing a new range of facial cleansers, and Golda knows that she will have a large volume of work the following day. In order to test all the samples before the end of the workday, she will need to come in early and focus only on testing the facial cleansers. Before leaving the lab, Golda makes sure she finishes paperwork related to another assignment. She knows she will not have time to work on it tomorrow, so she works hard to complete it by the end of the day. Later that evening, Golda sets her alarm an hour earlier and arrives at work before all of her coworkers. By the end of the day, she has tested and documented all the samples. She is able to leave on time to pick her son up from day care.

3. How do Golda's actions demonstrate her ability to prioritize?

   A. She foresees that she will have a larger than usual workload.

   B. She focuses on testing all of the samples and does not complete her other assignments.

   C. She works hard to complete her other tasks the day before so she can focus on testing the cleanser samples.

   D. She delegates most of her work to the other lab technicians so she will have time to test the cleanser samples.

   E. She stays later than usual to finish the samples.

4. What might have happened if Golda had not prioritized her tasks?

   F. She might have finished testing the samples early.

   G. She might have picked up her son on time and then brought him back to the lab to finish her work.

   H. She might not have been able to finish testing all the samples before the end of the day.

   J. She might have contaminated all the samples.

   K. She might have had to wake up even earlier.

Think About It Think about Marisol's and Golda's actions. What impression do you think each made on her supervisor? Which one of them is more likely to be viewed as an employee who manages her time effectively? In forming your answer, think about the following questions:

- **Responsibility** How did Marisol and Golda demonstrate time management skills or a lack of time management skills? What might the consequences of their actions be?

- **Solve Problems** What might have happened if Marisol and Golda had behaved differently? What can Marisol do in the future to manage her time more effectively?

Remember!

Manage Time Effectively It is important to plan ahead and prioritize your tasks according to deadlines and the importance of the task. The sooner something is due and the more important a task is, the higher up on your list of priorities it should be. In *Example 2,* Golda knew about her busy day ahead of time, so she planned and prioritized her time to get the job done. To help you keep track of important dates, set up reminders on your computer or write reminders in a calendar.

Try It Out! ■ ■ ■

Allocating Resources Jacques is a manager at a popular restaurant. Jacques has the following conversation with a customer who visits whenever he is in town.

> *JACQUES: It's great to see you again, Clive. When will you be in town next?*
> *CLIVE: Actually, I'll be back next month with the entire department. Our annual convention is being held at the hotel across the street.*
> *JACQUES: I hope we'll see you then.*
> *CLIVE: Absolutely. I've been telling everyone about the great food and wonderful service you have here. You can plan on a big crowd of hungry people!*

During weekdays, Jacques has only one chef and a handful of regular wait staff. He employs additional staff for busier times such as evenings and weekends. The conference will likely bring a lot of customers into the restaurant, and Jacques is concerned that he will be unable to cope with the additional demand.

Decision-Making Process				
STEP 1: Identify the Problem	**STEP 2:** Locate, Gather, and Organize Relevant Information	**STEP 3:** Generate Alternatives	**STEP 4:** Choose a Solution	**STEP 5:** Implement the Solution
Jacques is expecting a lot of customers during the conference and does not know if he can cope with the additional demand.	The conference next month is likely to bring large crowds to his restaurant. Jacques is unsure if his usual weekday staff can handle it.	Jacques can have his weekday employees work extra hard during the conference. Jacques can revise his schedule so that night and weekend employees also work days during the conference.	Jacques does not want to overwork or upset his staff, so he chooses to revise his schedule so that employees who usually work nights and weekends also work during the week of the conference.	Jacques meets with his staff to discuss their availability and creates a schedule for the week of the conference.

Jacques knows that the conference is likely to attract a lot of extra customers to the restaurant. One of his regular diners has already told him that he will be bringing an entire department the next time he visits. Jacques has a month to prepare for the conference. Jacques does not want to overwork his small weekday staff, so he decides to revise his staff schedule. This way, employees who usually work nights and weekends can help the regular weekday staff during the conference. Jacques meets with his staff to discuss availability and creates a schedule for the week of the conference. By planning ahead and reallocating resources, Jacques is able to handle the high demand from the conference.

Planning Sanibel is a network systems administrator. Her company has several large clients, and one of Sanibel's main responsibilities is to ensure that their computer networks are running smoothly. On Thursday morning, Sanibel receives the following voice mail from her supervisor, Doug.

> *Hi Sanibel, this is Doug. Listen, I just got a call from Ani at PetroTech. It seems their SQL server is down, and it needs to be fixed as soon as possible. Can you head over there first thing this morning and handle the problem? Give me a call when you're back in the office.*

Sanibel puts the phone down and immediately leaves for the PetroTech office on the other side of town. When she arrives, Ani directs her to the server she will be working on. Sanibel attempts to boot up the system and quickly realizes that she needs a particular SQL software package. Unfortunately, Sanibel left the software in her office and does not have it with her.

1. How might Sanibel's poor planning affect her client?
   A. Her client will be unable to access the server for an extended period of time.
   B. Her client will be happy with the service it received and recommend Sanibel's company to others.
   C. Her client will have to purchase a new SQL software package.
   D. Her client will have to purchase a new server.
   E. Her client will have to relocate to an office across town that has better connectivity.

2. What should Sanibel have done differently to plan for her task?
   F. She should have told her boss that she was not equipped for the task.
   G. She should have told the client that she would be unable to complete the task.
   H. She should have made sure she had everything she needed before leaving the office.
   J. She should have asked her coworker to complete the task for her.
   K. She should have told the client to order the software for the office.

Reflect Thinking through the steps in the *Decision-Making Process* can help you decide what course of action to take. Consider the actions of the employees in each of the *Try It Out!* examples. Do you think they made the correct decisions? What information did they take into consideration when making their decisions? What information would have been useful to take into consideration?

On Your Own ■ ■ ■

Read the following scenarios. Then answer the questions that follow each scenario.

SCENARIO A Anticipating Obstacles

As an agriculture manager for a small farm, you are in charge of the farm's day-to-day activities. Usually, you help out with some of the smaller jobs, such as fertilizing and spraying the crops.

> Harvest time is approaching, and you know that you will soon be very busy. You doubt that you will be able to help out with some of the smaller jobs on the farm. You will be busy doing bookkeeping, marketing produce, and organizing transportation to the farmers' market and stores. In fact, you are not sure if your current farmhands will be able to take on the extra work by themselves.

Complete the chart below and then answer the questions that follow.

Decision-Making Process				
STEP 1: Identify the Problem	**STEP 2:** Locate, Gather, and Organize Relevant Information	**STEP 3:** Generate Alternatives	**STEP 4:** Choose a Solution	**STEP 5:** Implement the Solution
You are unsure if you have enough staff to complete the daily tasks during harvest time.	During harvest time, you will be too busy with managerial tasks to help work in the fields.			

1. What are some possible solutions to this problem?

2. What are the positive and negative consequences of each solution you listed?

SCENARIO B Prioritizing

You are a newly hired housekeeper who works for a hotel. The hotel's policy is that housekeepers should prioritize which rooms they clean based on which rooms will be occupied that day.

> On your first day you decide that it would be more efficient to start on the bottom floor and work your way up. By midday you have cleaned only three floors. Guests will be checking in soon, and many rooms several floors up still need to be cleaned. You are unsure if you should keep working your way up or begin cleaning rooms on the priority list.

3. What is the problem with this situation?

4. What are some possible solutions to this problem? What are the pros and cons of each solution?

5. Which solution would demonstrate that you are able to prioritize your tasks?

SCENARIO C Planning

As a self-employed plumber, it is in your best interest to schedule as many clients as possible so you have steady business.

> You receive a call from a client regarding a blocked drain and schedule an appointment for 2 P.M. that day. Later, you get a call from a client in the same neighborhood who needs a plumber before 4 P.M. Usually, you leave a longer gap between appointments to account for potential problems. However, you decide to go ahead and book the appointment with the second client. When you arrive at the first client's house, you soon realize that she has a complicated drainage problem. There is no way you will make your 4 P.M. appointment.

6. What solution would you choose to implement?

7. Who, if anyone, would you need to communicate your solution to?

SCENARIO D Allocating Resources

You are the district manager for a small chain of copy shops. This morning, you have a voice mail from the store manager of one of your locations.

> *Hey, it's Calvin. We just received a large order that the customer needs by Friday. I just realized that we don't have enough colored ink to complete the order. If we order ink now, we won't receive it until Monday. Give me a call back so we can figure out what to do. I'll be at the shop until 4 P.M. Thanks!*

Another location just received an order of colored ink. You are not sure if you should send the ink to the store with the order or send the order to the store with the ink.

8. What alternative actions might you take in this situation?

9. Which solution would you choose to implement?

Summary ▪ ▪ ▪

Employees with good time-management skills complete tasks efficiently and on time. To ensure that you manage your time effectively, be sure to do the following:

- **Plan ahead** Look at your upcoming schedule to determine whether anything is happening that is likely to require additional time or resources.

- **Prioritize** Identify the most important tasks and tackle them first.

- **Allocate resources** Allocate sufficient resources to complete a task effectively.

- **Anticipate obstacles** Consider potential obstacles and plan how to avoid or work around them.

Answers begin on page 131.

Lesson 12 ■ ■ ■
Being Professional

Keeping up a professional manner can sometimes be difficult. However, it is a vital skill to master. Professional employees show self-control and keep a well-groomed appearance. They have a healthy work–life balance, and express a positive attitude no matter what their circumstances.

Skill Examples ■ ■ ■

Demonstrating Self-Control Renata works as a waitress and Herschel is a production worker. Renata interacts with dozens of customers each day, and Herschel works closely with several other employees. Both Renata and Herschel are occasionally angered by the actions of these other people.

Read the two examples and answer the questions that follow.

EXAMPLE 1 **Renata's Reaction**

> Renata is a waitress at a family restaurant. On a busy Saturday night, a large group sits in her section. The group members behave very rudely to Renata, clicking their fingers to get her attention and shouting at her from across the restaurant. When they finally leave, Renata notices that they have not left a tip. Her mood turns from bad to worse, and she begins behaving rudely toward her other customers. When a diner asks her to bring him some silverware, Renata tells him to get it himself and stomps into the kitchen.

1. What might happen to Renata as a result of her behavior?
   A. She will not be allowed to serve large groups of customers.
   B. She will make mistakes and deliver incomplete orders to her tables.
   C. She will be reprimanded and possibly fired.
   D. She will not receive tips from any of her tables that night.
   E. She will refuse to serve customers who do not tip.

2. How should Renata have behaved despite being frustrated?
   F. She should have calmed down and kept a positive attitude.
   G. She should have asked her new customers to tip her well.
   H. She should have asked her manager if she could leave early.
   J. She should have asked one of the other wait staff to cover her tables.
   K. She should have banned the large group from returning to the restaurant.

Remember!
Customer Relations
The way you interact with others affects how people view you. In *Example 1,* Renata allows a bad experience with a customer to affect the way she behaves at work. The bad experience causes her to be rude and unprofessional. As a result, her manager may see her as someone who cannot maintain self-control.

EXAMPLE 2 Herschel's Reaction

> Herschel is a plastics production worker. During the past few weeks, he has noticed that one of his coworkers, Lou, is not doing his share of the work. Herschel frequently catches Lou taking unauthorized breaks or chatting with other workers. Lou's production rate is well below average and his poor performance is affecting the whole shift. Herschel is very angry but manages to stay calm. He asks Lou if he can speak with him in private. Herschel explains his concerns and asks Lou to try to increase his rate.

3. How do Herschel's actions show that he is able to maintain his self-control?

   A. He does not take breaks.

   B. He speaks to Lou calmly and does not get angry.

   C. He has the highest production rate in the shift.

   D. He is in charge of all the other production workers.

   E. He does not waste time chatting with other workers.

4. What might have happened if Herschel had lost his temper and shouted at Lou?

   F. Herschel's words might have lost their effectiveness.

   G. Herschel might have demonstrated that he was in charge.

   H. Lou might have worked twice as hard in the future.

   J. Herschel might have been promoted to production manager.

   K. Lou might have been moved to another shift.

Think About It Think about Renata's and Herschel's behavior. What kind of impression do you think they made on their coworkers? Which one of them is more likely to be perceived as professional? In forming your answer, think about the following questions:

- **Interact Effectively with Others** How did Renata and Herschel interact with others, and how might this influence people's opinion of them?

- **Understand Systems** If Renata and Herschel continue to behave the same way, are they both likely to keep their jobs? What might happen if they behave differently?

Remember!

Self-Management You may arrive at work upset about a difficult commute or a problem at home. A situation at work might make you feel angry or frustrated. Regardless of the cause of these feelings, it is important to control your reactions and maintain a professional manner. In *Example 2,* Herschel is angry with his coworker. By approaching Lou calmly and speaking respectfully, Herschel makes his point without losing his self-control.

Try It Out! ■ ■ ■

Balancing Work and Life Rosette is a mortgage loan officer at a large bank. She assists customers with completing loan applications. Recently, the bank downsized, laying off employees. Rosette now has twice as many customers.

> Rosette is unable to fit all of her customers into a regular 40-hour week. She has trouble responding promptly to all of her customers, because of the many demands on her time. She frequently works in the evenings, staying late at the bank or bringing paperwork home with her. Many of her customers find the mortgage loan process confusing, and Rosette is constantly answering questions or trying to locate missing paperwork. She rarely gets to spend time with her family. She has even been late twice in the past week to pick up her son from day care.

Rosette enjoys her job, but she is exhausted. She is unable to maintain both her work and home responsibilities. Rosette knows that something has to change.

Decision-Making Process				
STEP 1: Identify the Problem	**STEP 2:** Locate, Gather, and Organize Relevant Information	**STEP 3:** Generate Alternatives	**STEP 4:** Choose a Solution	**STEP 5:** Implement the Solution
Rosette's work schedule is affecting her personal life.	Rosette cannot meet her customers' needs. Rosette frequently has to work late in the evenings. Rosette has been late picking up her son from day care.	Rosette can arrange to have a neighbor pick up her son from day care. Rosette can ask her manager to reduce the number of clients with which she works.	Rosette enjoys her job, but it is affecting her personal life. Having someone else pick up her son from day care will not solve the entire problem. She chooses to discuss the situation with her manager.	Rosette e-mails her manager and asks to schedule a meeting.

Rosette knows that her work schedule is negatively affecting her family life and work performance. She frequently has to stay late at the bank or bring work home with her. She is also often late picking up her son from day care. Her first option is to arrange for a friend to pick up her son from day care. However, this is only a short-term solution because she would still not achieve a realistic work-life balance. Her second option is to discuss reducing the number of clients with her manager. This would enable Rosette to better manage her schedule and spend more time with her family. Rosette e-mails her manager to arrange a meeting. Her manager agrees that her schedule has become unmanageable. He arranges to meet with her next week to discuss ways to resolve the situation.

Demonstrating Self-Control Miguel is a baker. He enjoys creating big cakes for special occasions such as birthdays or weddings, and often meets with clients to discuss their needs. On Thursday, he has a meeting with a bride-to-be about her wedding cake.

> CLIENT: I like the three-tier chocolate cake, but I'm not willing to pay more than $200 for it.
>
> MIGUEL: I'm terribly sorry ma'am, but I have set prices for my cakes. The three-tier cakes cost $350.
>
> CLIENT: Don't be ridiculous! No cake is worth $350. Are you trying to rip me off? What kind of business are you running here? Let me talk to a manager. I want a three-tier cake for $200 by next Wednesday, and it had better be perfect.

Miguel is shocked by the customer's rudeness and offended by her accusations. He is tempted to say something rude but manages to keep his temper in check. Miguel apologizes to the woman and tells her he will get his manager. Before leaving the customer with his manager, Miguel wishes her well with the rest of her wedding plans.

1. How might Miguel's actions affect his manager's opinion of him?
   - A. His manager might view him as rude and offensive.
   - B. His manager might view him as reasonable and in control.
   - C. His manager might view him as unprofessional.
   - D. His manager might view him as a poor decision maker.
   - E. His manager might view him as soft and easy to manipulate.

2. What might have happened if Miguel had lost his temper with the customer?
   - F. He might have been disciplined by his manager.
   - G. He might have caused the bakery to be shut down for poor service.
   - H. He might have received a good recommendation from the potential client.
   - J. He might have been rewarded by his manager for standing firm.
   - K. He might have agreed to make the wedding cake for $200.

Reflect In both of the *Try It Out!* examples, the employees made decisions about how to react to difficult situations in the workplace. What were the outcomes of their decisions? What other decisions could they have made, and how might the outcomes have been different?

Remember!

Customer Relations

Dealing with rude or unreasonable customers is a common undertaking for people in many industries and positions. Although demanding customers might upset you, keep smiling and remain calm. Miguel showed self-control by being polite to a rude customer. When a customer makes unreasonable demands, or makes a request that you are not authorized to meet, speak to a superior or refer the customer to your manager directly, as Miguel did. By keeping his temper under control and remaining polite, Miguel demonstrated good customer service skills and also ensured customer satisfaction.

On Your Own ▪ ■ ▪

Read the following scenarios. Then answer the questions that follow each scenario.

SCENARIO A Maintaining a Professional Appearance

You have recently been hired as a graphic designer. Usually, the office dress code is business casual, but you are expected to dress more formally when customers visit.

> Your boss sends out an e-mail on Friday afternoon informing you that an important client will be visiting the office on Monday afternoon. She asks you to dress formally to give a good first impression. On Monday morning, you are in a hurry and completely forget about the e-mail. You arrive at the office dressed in sneakers and jeans.

Complete the chart below and then answer the questions that follow.

Decision-Making Process				
STEP 1: Identify the Problem	**STEP 2:** Locate, Gather, and Organize Relevant Information	**STEP 3:** Generate Alternatives	**STEP 4:** Choose a Solution	**STEP 5:** Implement the Solution
You were asked to dress formally for an important client, but you arrive at the office in casual wear.	An important client is due in the office on Monday afternoon. You have specifically been asked to dress in formal wear.			

1. What are some alternative ways to solve this problem?

2. Who, if anyone, would you communicate your solution to? How would you communicate this to them?

SCENARIO B Demonstrating Self-Control

You are a technical writer for a software developer. On Thursday night, you invite a friend over for dinner and get into an argument. Your friend leaves your house very upset.

> On Friday morning, you receive several phone calls and text messages from your friend while you are in the office. You want to make up with your friend, but you have a lot of deadlines approaching.

3. What problem do you need to solve?

4. What are some possible solutions to this problem?

5. Which solutions would demonstrate that you are a professional employee?

SCENARIO C Maintaining a Positive Attitude

You are a sales associate for a home improvement store. Your manager has called a staff meeting to discuss ideas for a new holiday display.

> SUPERVISOR: As you know, Memorial Day is coming up. We need to figure out what to do for this year's display. Any suggestions?
> YOU: I think we should put a big Memorial Day display at the front entrance. We could wave flags and hand out buttons to encourage shoppers to enter the store.
> SUPERVISOR: That's a cute idea, but I don't think we have the budget to do that. Any other suggestions? No? Okay, this is what we're going to do. Let's put up a small display by the decorations aisle. Now, let's discuss the schedule…

You are disappointed that your idea was not chosen. At the end of the meeting, the manager places you in charge of setting up the display.

6. What is the problem for which you need to find a solution?

7. What alternative solutions could you take to resolve the problem?

8. Which solutions would show that you are a professional employee?

SCENARIO D Balancing Work and Life

You are a full-time student. To pay your tuition fees, you have a part-time position as a waitress at a popular off-campus restaurant.

> Your shift begins immediately after your last class, so you do not have time to return home first. As a result, you are unable to wash and iron your work uniform between shifts. Several times a week, you wear a shirt that is noticeably stained and crumpled.

9. What are some possible solutions to this problem?

10. Which solution would show that you have a healthy work–life balance?

Summary ▪ ▪ ▪

Behaving professionally at work demonstrates that you are a responsible and credible employee. To ensure that you are professional, be sure to do the following:

- **Demonstrate self-control** Remain calm and polite in all situations.

- **Maintain a professional appearance** Show up for work in appropriate attire.

- **Balance work and life** Ask for help if work typically affects your personal life.

- **Maintain a positive attitude** Carry out your tasks with a smile even when things do not go your way.

Answers begin on page 132.

Getting Ahead...

It is important to think of yourself as a professional and to find ways to grow in your job and career. Being proactive and self-motivated and developing new skills and strategies will help you achieve your goals and gain your employer's respect.

In Theme 4, you will learn about skills and behaviors that will better position you to get ahead.

Lesson 13: Being Self-Motivated Employees who are self-motivated achieve their goals and seek out challenges. *Objectives include*:

- Persisting
- Working Independently
- Setting Challenging Goals
- Achievement Motivation

Lesson 14: Dealing with Change Changes will happen in the workplace. Flexible employees will be able to adapt to new approaches. *Objectives include*:

- Dealing with Ambiguity
- Entertaining New Approaches
- Generating Creative Solutions

Lesson 15: Being a Good Learner Good learning means updating workplace skills, applying strategies, and being aware of changes. *Objectives include*:

- Participating in Training
- Applying Knowledge and Skills
- Anticipating Changes at Work
- Employing Learning Strategies

Lesson 16: Understanding Business Having business understanding requires an employee to see the big picture and understand his or her influence. *Objectives include*:

- Situational Awareness
- Market Knowledge
- Business Ethics

Key Factors for Getting Ahead ▪ ▪ ▪

These lessons are intended to help you identify and practice the behaviors necessary for getting ahead. Employees who purposefully improve themselves can prevent a lull in their careers. Employers value workers who want to get ahead. To better position yourself to get ahead in the workplace, you must be able to:

- **Solve problems** Employees may not be in a position to make decisions. However, by offering solutions to problems, employees can show their employer that they have good judgment.

- **Display self-esteem** Striving to improve is one way of showing that you take pride in yourself and your performance. Looking for new and more efficient ways of completing tasks, learning new skills, and asking for help shows that you take pride in your performance and want to improve.

- **Know how to learn** Understanding how to learn shows employers that you have the ability to expand your skills and grow with the company.

Working hard and being motivated will demonstrate that you want to get ahead. Employees who are proactive in learning new skills and strategies are more efficient, better able to achieve their goals, and more likely to advance in their careers.

Remember!

Getting ahead involves skills that you can practice, develop, and master. Motivation does not have to be an existing personality trait; rather, it can be a trait you concentrate on developing to ensure your success. Employers value employees who work hard to hone their own work habits.

Lesson 13
Being Self-Motivated

In any line of work, it is important to be self-motivated. People who are self-motivated are driven to achieve their goals and complete their tasks. Self-motivated employees are able to work independently; they are also able to persist when work is challenging. They set challenging goals for themselves and are motivated by their desire to achieve those goals.

Skill Examples

Persisting Jackson and Lavina are project managers at a thriving information technology company. They both have busy schedules and challenging workloads.

Read the two examples and answer the questions that follow.

EXAMPLE 1 Jackson's Heavy Workload

> As a project manager, Jackson has many responsibilities. He communicates with clients, tracks project requirements, and makes sure projects are completed on time and within the budget. His company recently acquired a new client. Jackson expects that his workload will increase. Jackson's supervisor, Mia, has asked him to contact the new client by the end of the week to discuss project requirements. Jackson plans to contact the client on Friday. By Friday, however, several urgent tasks have come up. Since he does not want to work late, Jackson tries to finish these tasks before calling the client. It is 5 P.M. by the time he has completed his work. Jackson knows that the client call could take awhile. He decides to make the call on Monday so he does not have to stay late on a weekend night.

1. What might be the consequences of Jackson's actions?
   A. Jackson might have to work on the weekend.
   B. The company might praise Jackson for his actions.
   C. Other clients might request that the company make Jackson the project manager for their projects.
   D. The company might decide to give Jackson more work.
   E. The client might be upset that no one from Jackson's company has been in touch.

2. What could Jackson have done to show his initiative to complete his tasks?
   F. He could have let Mia know he was too busy to call the client.
   G. He could have called the client and then stayed late if necessary to finish the other tasks.
   H. He could have completed the other tasks on Monday and called the client on Friday.
   J. He could have told the client that he could not talk to him until Monday.
   K. He could have asked Mia to do his other tasks while he called the client.

EXAMPLE 2 Lavina's Busy Schedule

Lavina is a project manager. Her company has just acquired a new client and assigned Lavina to work with that client. This will mean her schedule will be busier than normal. Every night before she leaves work, Lavina makes a list of tasks to complete the following day. She works through lunch occasionally. She also works late when necessary to complete her tasks. On Thursday afternoon, Lavina's supervisor, Tracy, asks her to be sure to send a project schedule to her new client this week. Lavina knows her schedule for Friday is already packed with obligations—including a lunchtime meeting. In addition, she has to pick up her daughter from day care. Lavina recognizes that working with a new client requires some extra time up front. She is also aware that her schedule will be back to normal next week. Lavina decides to make arrangements with friends or family so that someone else can pick up her daughter from day care if she needs to work late.

3. What might the consequences of Lavina's actions be for her?
  A. She might be reprimanded for putting in extra hours.
  B. She might resent her job and eventually quit.
  C. She might be disliked by her colleagues for working too hard.
  D. She might be able to complete her tasks on time.
  E. She might be exhausted on Friday and late to pick up her daughter.

4. What would probably have happened if Lavina had not made the necessary arrangements that would allow her to work late?
  F. She would have been able to take on extra work.
  G. She would have had to work through lunch.
  H. She would have been able to complete the schedule a day earlier.
  J. She would not have been able to complete her tasks.
  K. She would have been admired for taking care of her personal affairs.

Think About It Think about Jackson's and Lavina's actions. Which one of them is more likely to be trusted with greater responsibilities in the future? In forming your answer, think about the following questions:

  ▪ **Responsibility** How did Jackson and Lavina display or not display initiative in accomplishing their tasks?

  ▪ **Solve Problems** What might have happened if Jackson and Lavina had told their supervisors that they needed help to handle their workloads?

Remember!

Responsibility It is important to maintain a high standard of quality when completing assigned tasks. It shows your level of responsibility toward your job. In *Example 2*, Lavina carefully keeps track of her schedule and tasks to make sure she is able to complete all her assignments. She makes alternate arrangements to take care of her personal commitments so that she is able to work extra hours when needed.

Try It Out! ■ ■ ■

Working Independently Roger works as a medical transcriptionist. He listens to recordings from physicians and transcribes their words into print for medical records and related documents. Many of the terms he hears in the recordings are unfamiliar to him. Roger does not have a background in medicine. However, reference materials are available at the office where he works. Roger is currently working on transcribing the following recording.

> A 42-year-old male came into the ER complaining of severe angina. I took patient's history and ordered ECG, blood and urine tests, and chest X-ray. Patient has a myocardial infarction. Patient has a history of ischemic heart disease. Patient is found to have coronary atherosclerosis with heavy plaque deposits.

Roger is not familiar with some of the terms used by the doctor. He has heard of *ECG* but is not certain what it stands for. He knows the patient visited the emergency room and has a history of heart disease. However, words like *plaque deposits* seem to relate to dental issues, not heart disease. *Atherosclerosis* is another unfamiliar term. Roger wants to make sure he correctly spells all of the terms he hears.

Decision-Making Process

STEP 1: Identify the Problem	STEP 2: Locate, Gather, and Organize Relevant Information	STEP 3: Generate Alternatives	STEP 4: Choose a Solution	STEP 5: Implement the Solution
Roger is not sure how to spell some of the terms he hears in the doctor's recording. He also does not know what a particular abbreviation stands for.	Roger does not have a background in medicine. Medical reference materials are available to Roger.	Roger can ask his supervisor to find the information he needs. Roger can look up terms in a medical reference book.	Roger chooses to use a company-approved medical reference book.	Roger selects a reference book with information about heart disease.

Roger wants to type the transcript accurately, but he is not familiar with all the terms in the recording. Roger's first option is to ask his supervisor for help, but his supervisor is busy and does not have time to deal with issues that are not urgent. Roger decides to use a company-approved reference instead. He looks through the available materials and selects one that is likely to have relevant information. Roger is able to use the book to check the spelling of unfamiliar terms and the meaning of *ECG*. Roger's actions show that he cares about accuracy and can independently make use of available resources.

Remember!

Solving Problems
Whenever possible, try to solve problems or answer questions yourself before asking for assistance. If you then realize you cannot solve the problem alone, ask your supervisor to help you. In the *Try It Out!* example on this page, had Roger not been able to find the information he needed in a reference book, he could have asked his supervisor to listen to the recording. He also could have asked about other reference materials he might use to find the answers to his questions.

Setting Challenging Goals Amina is a baker. At the local bakery where she works, she handles all of her assigned tasks successfully, except for decorating specialty cakes. Her boss usually assigns decorating duties to other employees.

> From past experience, Amina knows the bakery gets a large quantity of orders for specialty cakes during the spring and summer. Many customers place orders for graduation cakes and wedding cakes. It is a hectic time for the bakery. Employees on "decorating duty" are especially busy. Amina feels frustrated that she is not asked to participate in decorating the specialty cakes. She also worries that her coworkers will resent her for not helping. It is now early May and the busy season will begin soon.

Amina decides to tell her manager that she is tired of only baking bread and pies. She demands that she be allowed to help decorate cakes during this busy season, or she will quit.

1. How might Amina's manager respond to her demand to decorate cakes?
   A. Amina's manager might allow her to decorate cakes and risk losing some customers.
   B. Amina's manager might be thrilled because he has one more person to help during a busy time.
   C. Amina's manager might be upset because he has already chosen the best people for the job and Amina has to learn to work as part of the team.
   D. Amina's manager might admire her for daring to make such a demand.
   E. Amina's manager might decide not to allow customers to order specialty cakes anymore.

2. What could Amina have done differently to solve the problem?
   F. She could have planned on improving her skills so that she was ready to help during the busy season.
   G. She could have insisted that customers do not care if their cakes are not decorated perfectly.
   H. She could have tried to convince customers to buy her baked goods instead of ordering cakes.
   J. She could have asked her boss to not offer specialty cakes anymore.
   K. She could have passed off the cakes that were decorated by her coworkers as her own.

Reflect In both of the *Try It Out!* examples, the employees had to decide how to solve a problem. While Roger decided to use company-approved reference material to verify the spelling of unfamiliar terms, Amina told her boss that she was tired of baking bread and pies and demanded to help decorate specialty cakes during the busy season. Do you think they showed good judgment? Do their actions show that they know when to make independent decisions and when to ask for help? What other actions could they have taken to solve their problems and achieve their goals? How might these alternative actions have resulted in different outcomes?

Remember!

Monitor and Correct Performance Everyone has weaknesses. Successful employees turn their weaknesses into opportunities to learn more and improve their performance. You might take job-related classes, read material about an unfamiliar topic, or decide to learn a new skill on your own. If you want to expand your skills by taking on a new task at your job, be sure to communicate this to your supervisor. In the *Try It Out!* example on this page, Amina could have turned her weakness of not knowing how to decorate cakes into an opportunity if she had worked with her manager to meet her goal. Together they could have created a plan so that she learned to decorate cakes in time for the busy season.

On Your Own ▪ ▪ ▪

Read the following scenarios. Then answer the questions that follow each scenario.

SCENARIO A Setting Challenging Goals

You work as an assistant at a hair salon. Your long-term goal is to become a stylist. You ask one of the stylists you work with what is involved in pursuing this career.

> *The first thing you need to do is get certified. No reputable salon would employ a stylist who does not have a license. It takes about a year to a year and a half to complete the required course work. I got my license out of state, so I'm not sure where classes are offered around here.*

Complete the chart below and then answer the questions that follow.

Decision-Making Process				
STEP 1: Identify the Problem	**STEP 2:** Locate, Gather, and Organize Relevant Information	**STEP 3:** Generate Alternatives	**STEP 4:** Choose a Solution	**STEP 5:** Implement the Solution
You would like to become a stylist, but you do not have information about the necessary training.	Good salons hire only licensed stylists. Your coworker does not know about classes offered locally.			

1. Identify ways you could gather more information to solve the problem.

2. Which solution shows that you are working to achieve your goals?

SCENARIO B Persisting

As a floor and tile installer, you have been contracted to remodel a yoga studio and weight room for a health club. You are working on the flooring in the yoga studio.

> You planned to finish the yoga studio this week and then begin working on the weight room. However, your flooring supplier informed you that your shipment would be delayed. You have all of the materials you need for the weight room. Since you cannot finish the yoga studio until the flooring arrives, you consider what you should do next.

3. What is the problem that you need to solve?

4. What are some possible ways you could solve this problem?

5. Which solution would allow you to continue your work despite the obstacle presented by the delayed shipment?

SCENARIO C Working Independently

You have worked for five years as a hospital billing clerk. You have developed your own systems for performing tasks. As a result, you can do these tasks very efficiently.

> Your supervisor gives you a large stack of medical records to code for billing. She expects that this task will take a full day. However, thanks to your familiarity with specific codes, you can work quickly. By 1:00 P.M., you have finished the task. You have other tasks that you can complete, but you are not sure if your supervisor has more important work that needs your attention.

6. What are your alternatives in this situation?

7. Which alternative would ensure that your day is as productive as possible?

8. What information should you communicate to your supervisor?

SCENARIO D Achievement Motivation

As a high school math teacher, you enjoy working with your students. Although you are required to be at school until 3:00 P.M., you usually stay until 4:00 P.M. to tutor students. Recently, one of your students approached you to ask for extra help.

> One of your students has a C- in your calculus class. He approaches you to ask for help. He has football practice every day until 4:00 P.M., so he cannot meet with you during your tutoring time. He is willing to meet before school or on a weekend. If his grades do not improve, he will have to quit the football team.

9. What is one way you could solve this problem?

10. How might your actions demonstrate your "achievement motivation?"

Summary ▪ ▪ ▪

Employees who are self-motivated work through difficult periods and seek out new challenges. To become a self-motivated professional, make sure you do the following:

- **Persist** Find ways to continue your work and complete tasks even when obstacles arise. Be willing to put in extra effort when needed.

- **Set challenging goals** Think of short- and long-term goals to improve your performance, knowledge, and skills.

- **Work independently** Try to complete tasks on your own and use available resources before seeking help from others.

- **Achieve motivation** When making day-to-day decisions, think about what choices will provide you with a lasting feeling of accomplishment.

Answers begin on page 133.

Lesson 14 ■ ■ ■
Dealing with Change

It is important to be flexible and creative in a professional setting. Employees who successfully deal with change know how to entertain new approaches to doing business. When one solution to a problem does not work, they generate new solutions. When something is ambiguous, they seek more information.

Skill Examples ■ ■ ■

Dealing with Ambiguity Cesar and Chang both work as auto mechanics. Sometimes it can be difficult to identify the cause of a customer's car troubles.

Read the two examples and answer the questions that follow.

EXAMPLE 1 **Cesar's Difficult Repair**

> A customer brings his car to Cesar, complaining that the vehicle starts shaking when driven at highway speeds. Cesar believes that the problem is a vacuum leak at the side of the engine. In his two years of experience as a mechanic, he has frequently come across this problem. Cesar finds and repairs the leak. A week later, the customer returns and says the vehicle is still shaking at high speeds. The customer suggests there might be some other cause. Cesar dismisses this possibility. "No, it was definitely the vacuum leak, which I already fixed," he says. "Any other mechanic will tell you the same thing."

1. How is the customer most likely to react based on Cesar's behavior?
   A. He will thank Cesar for fixing the problem.
   B. He will agree that the problem is fixed.
   C. He will be angry at Cesar for refusing to help.
   D. He will offer Cesar extra money to fix the problem.
   E. He will ask Cesar to show him how to fix a vacuum leak.

2. What is another action that Cesar could have taken to respond to the customer's problem?
   F. He could have told the customer it would cost him more money for another repair.
   G. He could have suggested that the customer buy a new car.
   H. He could have examined the car for other problems that may have caused the shaking.
   J. He could have asked the customer to repair the car himself.
   K. He could have called other mechanics to prove that the vacuum leak was the most likely cause.

Remember!

Sociability Accept that you will occasionally make mistakes on the job, and do not assume that you are always right. Give your clients and customers the benefit of the doubt. Most of them will be reasonable with you in turn. In *Example 1,* Cesar is unwilling to explore other possible causes of the car problem, even though the customer says that he is still having a problem. This makes Cesar appear arrogant and uninterested in helping the customer.

EXAMPLE 2 Chang's Difficult Repair

A customer brings her car to Chang for a repair. She explains that lately she has been hearing a strange noise coming from the engine. Chang asks her to describe the sound more specifically, and she says it is a knocking sound. Chang knows this can happen when the car is low on oil, so he asks when the customer last had the oil changed. She says she had it changed just last week. Later, Chang checks for oil leaks and finds none. He also checks the oil pump to see if it is clogged, but he finds no problems. He realizes that low oil is not an issue. After checking out a few other possibilities, Chang finally determines that several rod bearings are worn and loose. He replaces them, and the problem is fixed.

3. Which of Chang's actions show that he is both flexible and persistent?

   A. After hearing about the problem, he immediately suspects the cause.

   B. He does not explore the problem until the customer describes the noise.

   C. He replaces the worn and loose rod bearings.

   D. He considers and explores multiple possibilities until he finds the problem's cause.

   E. He initially assumes the problem is that the customer did not get the oil changed recently.

4. What might have happened if Chang had insisted that low oil was the cause of the problem?

   F. He might have fixed the car more quickly.

   G. He might have proved that he knew more than his peers at the shop.

   H. He might have found and fixed many other problems with the car.

   J. He might have impressed his customer with his understanding of cars.

   K. He might never have figured out what was causing the knocking noise.

Think About It Both Cesar and Chang faced a situation where the cause of the problem and the solution were unclear. Think about how each responded. Which mechanic succeeded in fixing the car? Which customer is more likely to be satisfied? In forming your answer, think about the following questions:

- **Solve Problems** What did Cesar and Chang do differently in dealing with a customer and solving a problem? Which approach was more effective?

- **Monitor and Correct Performance** Should either mechanic change his approach? If so, how?

Remember!

Solve Problems

Sometimes the solution to a problem is not easy or obvious. When this is the case, do not give up. Seek out more information to help you think of new ideas and explanations. In *Example 2*, Chang first thinks that low oil is the cause of the shaking. When his initial idea proves to be incorrect, he continues to investigate the problem and look for solutions.

Try It Out! ■ ■ ■

Entertaining New Approaches Sarita works as a payroll clerk for a growing retail chain. Each week she must complete payroll data by Wednesday so employees can be paid on Thursday. As the company has grown, it has become harder for Sarita to complete her tasks on time. Last week, paychecks were issued late. Her manager left her the following voice mail.

> *Sarita, I am not sure what the problem was with last week's paychecks. What I do know is that this is unacceptable. The checks must go out every Thursday without exception. I know we are busy, but hiring another payroll clerk is not possible right now. With Kelly handling time sheets and you handling payroll data, we should not be experiencing these problems. Please let me know what we can do to make sure this does not happen again.*

Sarita does not have enough time to complete the payroll data. However, employees must get paid on time. She learns about a program that allows employees to enter their time sheets into a computer system. This would get her payroll data sooner. However, Sarita is unsure how to proceed.

Decision-Making Process				
STEP 1: Identify the Problem	**STEP 2:** Locate, Gather, and Organize Relevant Information	**STEP 3:** Generate Alternatives	**STEP 4:** Choose a Solution	**STEP 5:** Implement the Solution
Sarita does not have enough time to complete payroll data each week.	Hiring another employee is not possible. Checks must be issued on Thursdays. Sarita is aware of a software program that could help.	Sarita can stay late to complete her tasks. Sarita can inform her manager about the software program and find out if they can purchase it and use it.	Sarita chooses to inform her manager about the new software program.	Sarita informs her manager about the new software program and asks if they can buy it and use it.

Sarita is not able to complete her payroll tasks in one day. However, the company cannot hire another payroll clerk. Sarita is aware of a software program that allows employees to enter their time sheets into a computer system. This would get her the information sooner. Also, if Kelly is not processing time sheets, she will be free to help with payroll data as an additional benefit. Sarita considers working in the same way as always and staying late to complete her tasks. Alternatively, she could inform her manager about the software program and find out if they can purchase it. After thinking about the problem, Sarita meets with her manager and shares her information about the program. She asks if they can buy the program and use it in order to be able to issue paychecks on time.

Remember!

Monitor and Correct Performance

Sometimes, your usual system for completing a task may no longer succeed because of a change at your workplace. When this happens, think of ways you can modify your system or methods. Look closely at the process and identify ways to improve it. In the *Try It Out!* example on this page, Sarita finds that following her usual system for getting paychecks ready makes it tough for her to issue the checks on time. She informs her manager about a software program that would allow her to complete her tasks faster. Sarita asks her manager if they could purchase the program and use it so that she could be more efficient in her work.

Entertaining New Approaches Maor is a customer-service supervisor at a small online retailer. As part of his job, he prepares schedules, trains employees, and develops work procedures. He also communicates with management to solve problems. His team fields many telephone calls about routine order information. Many customers call with shipping questions such as the one below.

> Hi, I'm calling about the DVDs I ordered on March 27. My order number was A-35412. Could you tell me when my order will ship? Will it arrive in time for my daughter's birthday on April 6? Also, what is the total charge for shipping and handling?

Maor's team can find this information easily using tracking software. Maor thinks that customers should have access to the same information on the website. That way, his team could focus on more important issues. Maor believes that responding to such calls lowers productivity. For now, however, he wants his team to handle each call to the customer's satisfaction.

1. Which of the following is a potential consequence of Maor's current approach to the problem?
   A. Maor may blame his employees for wasting time.
   B. Customers may not obtain the order information they need.
   C. Customers may not receive their orders on time.
   D. Customers with serious problems may have to wait longer to receive help.
   E. Maor may not learn how to use tracking software effectively.

2. What would most likely happen if Maor were to implement the new approach?
   F. His team would be flooded with calls about routine shipping information.
   G. His team would be able to focus on more important customer problems.
   H. His company would have to hire more customer-service representatives.
   J. His team would require training in how to use the company website.
   K. His company would receive complaints regarding poor service.

Reflect In both of the *Try It Out!* examples, employees had to decide what approach to use in addressing a known problem. Sarita told her supervisor about a new program that could help her work faster and get paychecks ready on time. Maor, on the other hand, did not discuss the issue with his supervisor. Do you think the approaches they chose were effective? What effect did their decisions have on their coworkers, customers, and respective companies?

Remember!

Responsibility Take responsibility to complete tasks assigned to you. Part of being responsible and doing your job well is to improve your work process. Make an effort to work as efficiently as possible by minimizing cost and time. By not suggesting improvements, Maor may be costing the company extra time and risking angering customers who have to wait longer to talk to a service representative. In other words, he is failing in his responsibilities to provide excellent customer service.

On Your Own ▪ ▪ ▪

Read the following scenarios. Then answer the questions that follow each scenario.

SCENARIO A Dealing with Ambiguity

You are a hotel manager. One of your responsibilities is to plan for hotel events.

> Next Saturday, the hotel is hosting an important event. A popular self-help author and media personality will be staying at the hotel. She will be signing copies of her books and then speaking before a group. You are supposed to provide refreshments. However, you do not know how much food and drink to order, because you do not know how many people are attending. The event's attendees registered with the speaker's event-planning team, not the hotel.

Complete the chart below and then answer the questions that follow.

Decision-Making Process				
STEP 1: Identify the Problem	**STEP 2:** Locate, Gather, and Organize Relevant Information	**STEP 3:** Generate Alternatives	**STEP 4:** Choose a Solution	**STEP 5:** Implement the Solution
You are unsure of how much food and drink to order because you do not know how many people are attending.	You do not know how many people are attending. Attendees have registered with the speaker's event-planning team.			

1. What are some alternatives for how to proceed in this situation?

2. Whom do you need to communicate with to implement your chosen solution?

SCENARIO B Entertaining New Approaches

You work as a dental hygienist. Occasionally you find it difficult to find a patient's records because they were incorrectly filed.

> You need to find the file for a patient with the last name of Johnson. You search for it in the filing cabinet, becoming increasingly frustrated. You believe the office's paper filing system is inefficient. You also believe your supervisor agrees with you on this point. You would prefer an electronic filing system. However, your supervisor says the office cannot afford it.

3. What information do you have available about this problem?

4. What are some ways you could try to solve this problem?

5. Which solution would show that you can generate creative solutions? Why?

SCENARIO C Generating Creative Solutions

As the owner of a driving school, you would like to market the school using social media. You have some familiarity with social media. However, you are not sure how it is used by high school students, who provide much of your business.

> You decide to find out more about social media. You know that one of your teenage nieces uses social media sites to market her handmade jewelry. As you do research online, you come across a marketing company's website. They claim to be on the cutting edge of social-media marketing. Most of their clients are large corporations.

6. What problem do you need to solve?

7. What are some possible solutions to this problem?

8. Which solution would you choose to implement? Why?

SCENARIO D Generating Creative Solutions

As a caterer, you are in charge of food and beverages for a fund-raiser next week. A few days before the event, you receive a voice mail from your produce supplier.

> *Hi, I'm calling about your order of lemons for the fund-raiser. Our shipment of lemons is delayed. We get our stock from Florida, and the bad weather there has delayed shipments. We won't have any lemons in until next week.*

Your client has specifically requested lemon meringue pie for dessert. Now that your order of lemons is not likely to be available in time, you have to think of other options.

9. What alternative actions might you take, and what might their consequences be?

10. To whom will you need to communicate your solution?

Summary ▪ ▪ ▪

Employees who are adaptable and flexible deal with change successfully. To ensure that you are flexible and adaptable, be sure you are doing the following:

- **Generating creative solutions** Understand that your first idea may not work. Keep trying until you find a solution for the problem.

- **Entertaining new approaches** Recognize when a given system or approach is not effective. Do not be afraid to suggest an improvement.

- **Dealing with ambiguity** Accept that sometimes the cause of a problem is not obvious. Take the time to explore multiple possibilities.

Answers begin on page 134.

Lesson 15
Being a Good Learner

Most jobs require that you update your skills regularly. Employees who are good learners apply the knowledge and skills they already have and make use of learning strategies. They participate in available training. They also anticipate and prepare for changes at work.

Skill Examples

Participating in Training Jamal and Amar both have jobs in which they work with industry-specific tools, and often, new tools are introduced. Each employee has been given an opportunity to learn about new tools that will help them with their work.

Read the two examples and answer the questions that follow.

EXAMPLE 1 **Jamal's Training**

> Jamal works as a glazier for a construction company. His job involves choosing, cutting, installing, and removing glass for items such as windows, shower doors, and mirrors. Recently, a new tool for cutting glass has come on the market. The manufacturer of the tool sends a representative to Jamal's company to conduct an optional training session. Although Jamal's company has not yet purchased the new tool, he thinks it would be good for him to learn about it now. That way he will be ready to use the tool when it becomes available. Jamal decides to attend the session. Later, he talks with his supervisor, Marcus, about what he learned.

1. How might Jamal's actions influence Marcus's opinion of him?
   A. He might think Jamal is trying to show off how much he knows.
   B. He might think Jamal is not paying enough attention to his current projects.
   C. He might think Jamal cares about keeping his skills up to date.
   D. He might think Jamal is too eager to start using the new cutting tool.
   E. He might think Jamal wants to leave his job and go work for the manufacturer of the new tool.

2. What would have happened if Jamal had decided not to attend the training?
   F. His supervisor would have praised Jamal for not wasting time on unnecessary training.
   G. He would have been able to train his coworkers on how to use the tool.
   H. He would never have been able to learn to use the tool.
   J. He would have missed an opportunity to stay current with new technology in his field.
   K. He would have learned about the different uses of the tool.

Remember!

Use Technology

When new technology is developed for your industry, take the time to learn about it. Doing so can keep you up to date about the developments in your field and can help you improve your job or performance. It can also give you a competitive edge over your coworkers. In *Example 1*, Jamal attends the training session even though his company has yet to purchase the new tool. If this new tool is better than what his company is currently using, Jamal can recommend to his manager that they consider purchasing it.

EXAMPLE 2 Amar's Seminar

Amar is a printmaker for a small print shop. The shop designs one-of-a-kind posters and flyers. Amar sometimes creates prints with a printing press, working with inked metal plates to transfer images to paper. In recent years, the press has also begun creating digital prints using computer software. Amar sometimes works with these tools, too. The print shop's owner has decided to purchase a new printing press. The shop is offering three optional seminars on how to use the new equipment. Amar thinks he will not have trouble with it, so he does not attend any of the seminars. When the new press arrives, Amar struggles to operate it correctly. His prints come out poorly. He often has to stay late to complete his projects. He comes in on his days off to review the operating manual and practice using the new press.

3. Which of Amar's actions shows that he takes responsibility for learning?
    A. He creates prints using a printing press with metal plates.
    B. He sometimes works with digital printmaking software.
    C. He skips the seminar because he knows a great deal about printing.
    D. He stays late to complete his printing projects.
    E. He uses his days off to practice working with the machine.

4. What might have happened if Amar had attended one of the seminars?
    F. He might have upset his supervisor by not focusing on his work.
    G. He might have lost a valuable opportunity to update his knowledge about his field.
    H. He might have learned how to print using inked metal plates.
    J. He might have been able to use the new press quickly and effectively.
    K. He might have been forced to attend the remaining two seminars.

Think About It Consider the choices Jamal and Amar made about participating in training. What impression do you think their choices made on their employers? How might their choices benefit or harm them in the future? In forming your answer, think about the following questions:

- **Know How to Learn** How did Jamal and Amar react differently when given the opportunity to attend training?

- **Acquire and Use Information** What consequences could Jamal's and Amar's decisions have for them and for their companies?

Remember!

Know How to Learn
When change is a few weeks or months away, preparing for it might not seem important. However, successful employees think ahead. Make it a habit to do so. Even if you do not want to attend training right now, doing so may help you in the long run, because it will advance your skills. In *Example 2*, Amar's decision to skip training affects his performance. By practicing on his own time, Amar can eventually learn to use the new press, but because he is unprepared, the quality of his work is not as good. This costs the company time and money. Additionally, his coworkers who attended the seminar are better prepared than him and are hence more likely to receive promotions or raises. Participating in the seminar would have been an easier way to learn.

Try It Out! ■ ■ ■

Applying Knowledge and Skills Liesel works as an administrative assistant in a congresswoman's office. One of Liesel's colleagues, Andrew, is having trouble using a software program for mass mailings.

> *Liesel, can you help me figure out this software program? We're preparing flyers to mail to every residence in the congresswoman's district. I need to make sure they are addressed correctly, but I keep getting an error message. It says the database is not accessible, and the Help menu is not very helpful. I'm worried that I'm not going to get the flyers addressed by the end of the week.*

Liesel is not only familiar with the program Andrew is using, but she is also an expert at it. She wants to try to help Andrew. However, she is working on a few assignments of her own. One of these assignments is due at the end of the day, and she needs a half day to complete it. She is unsure of what she should do.

Decision-Making Process				
STEP 1: Identify the Problem	**STEP 2:** Locate, Gather, and Organize Relevant Information	**STEP 3:** Generate Alternatives	**STEP 4:** Choose a Solution	**STEP 5:** Implement the Solution
Liesel wants to help Andrew but is concerned about meeting her own deadlines.	Andrew is having trouble with the software. Liesel has used this software program and is an expert at it. One of Liesel's assignments is due at the end of the day and will take half of the day to complete.	Liesel can work on her own assignments and let Andrew figure out how to use the software. Liesel can help Andrew in the morning and work on her own assignment in the afternoon.	Liesel wants to help Andrew but does not want to neglect her own work. She chooses to offer to help Andrew but explains her own situation.	Liesel tells Andrew that she will help him in the morning but that she is unavailable in the afternoon because she has a deadline to meet.

Liesel wants to help Andrew. However, she also wants to make sure her own assignment is completed on time. Her first option is to focus on her own work, but that would not be helpful to Andrew. Since her most immediate deadline is at the end of the day and she can complete the task in half a day, she decides she can spare some time to assist Andrew. She explains the situation to him so he understands that her time is limited. She is able to find the error in the software quickly. Her choice to help Andrew has several benefits. She has taught Andrew about the software. This will in turn help Andrew complete his task on time. Additionally, the office benefits because work is completed on time.

Remember!

Work with Others

If you have the skills to complete a task, share your knowledge with your coworkers even if the task has not been assigned to you. For example, Liesel helps Andrew learn to use the software. This helps Andrew improve his performance and ensures that the goals of the office are met in a timely and effective manner.

Anticipating Changes at Work Sharif is the store manager at a local branch of a national electronics store. He is in charge of day-to-day staffing decisions. Recently, the company decided to install new cash registers. Sharif received the following e-mail from a representative of the software company.

○ ○ ○   **E-mail Message**

To: Sharif_Amat@elec.com

Subject: New Registers

Sharif,

The new cash registers will be installed in your store next Friday evening. If you would like us to train your employees on the new machines, please let me know and we can schedule an appointment. Thank you.

Sharif makes note of when the new registers will be installed but does not think it necessary to schedule training. He feels that there is not much difference in how cash registers operate and believes his team can handle the new machines without a problem. As usual, Sharif schedules five employees to work on Saturday, the day after the registers are installed. They have trouble operating the machines, leaving customers angry about the slow service.

1. Which of the following resulted from Sharif's decision?
   A. His employees learned the software quickly through the training.
   B. Customers were angry about the slow service.
   C. His employees resented having to attend the training.
   D. His branch of the store was the only one that used the new machines.
   E. His employees saved the company time and money by not attending the training session.

2. What should Sharif have done differently to prepare for the change?
   F. He should have scheduled mandatory training for all his employees and informed customers about a possible delay during checkout.
   G. He should have requested that employees from other branches who were familiar with the new machines be transferred to his store.
   H. He should have requested customers to help his staff use the new registers.
   J. He should have disciplined the employee who missed the training.
   K. He should have posted a notice explaining that the store would be closed that day.

Reflect In both of the *Try It Out!* examples, the employees had to choose a course of action. Did their decisions help other people learn? How did their decisions affect other employees and the organization as a whole? Did they apply their own knowledge and skills? Were they prepared to manage a new situation effectively?

Remember!

Solve Problems
Every job occasionally involves change, whether it is learning new technology or taking on new responsibilities. Understand that when you are adapting to change, your productivity may temporarily slow down. This is normal, because it takes time to adjust to change. In the *Try It Out!* example on this page, Sharif fails to predict and address problems caused by a change in the systems used. He does not recognize that his staff will require training on the new machines. As a result, he fails to expect a delay in providing service to his customers, which in turn angers and upsets them.

On Your Own ▪ ▪ ▪

Read the following scenarios. Then answer the questions that follow each scenario.

SCENARIO A **Applying Knowledge and Skills**

As an electrician, you maintain power systems for businesses and factories. For your own reference, you maintain a spreadsheet with tips on how to fix difficult problems.

> You receive a call from a factory manager about a power outage. When you arrive at the site, you learn that the neighboring buildings have power. Therefore, the problem is not with the main power line. As you inspect the electrical system, you realize that there is a wiring problem. A few months ago, you fixed a similar problem, but you do not remember how you fixed it.

Complete the chart below and then answer the questions that follow.

Decision-Making Process				
STEP 1: Identify the Problem	**STEP 2:** Locate, Gather, and Organize Relevant Information	**STEP 3:** Generate Alternatives	**STEP 4:** Choose a Solution	**STEP 5:** Implement the Solution
There is a power outage in a factory caused by a wiring problem that you have fixed before, but you cannot remember how you fixed it.	The main power line has not caused the outage. You maintain notes on how you have fixed difficult problems.			

1. What are some of your options for addressing this problem?

2. What option would you choose? Why?

SCENARIO B **Anticipating Changes at Work**

You work as a seafood packager. Shrimp season, your busiest time of year, is starting. Last year, you were unable to work extra hours because you had to pick up your son from day care. This year you want to make alternate plans so you can work the extra hours. You received the following voice mail from your supervisor.

> *As you know shrimp season is here and we're going to be very busy. I'm anticipating that we will all need to put in extra hours. Starting next month, can you work in the evening to help us get out all the shipments on time? Any delay on our part would lose us both customers and money.*

3. What are some possible ways you could respond to this voice mail? What are their potential consequences?

4. How will you choose to respond to this voice mail? Why?

SCENARIO C Employing Learning Strategies

As an administrative assistant at an insurance company, you complete various office tasks. However, you cannot create slide show presentations. You are worried that your more knowledgeable coworkers are being promoted ahead of you.

> One morning, your coworker, Debra, seems stressed. She tells you that your supervisor has just asked her to put together a fifteen-slide presentation. This task is fairly easy, but she has other work to do. She thinks she will have to stay late. You would like to help, but you do not know how to create slide shows.

5. What are some ways you could try to solve this problem?

6. Which solution would show that you know how to employ learning strategies?

SCENARIO D Participating in Training

As a writer for a local newspaper, you have used the same word-processing software for years. However, the paper will soon be switching over to a different program. One of your colleagues discusses his concerns about the change.

> *I've heard that Page Creator is completely different than our current program. I'm worried I'll have trouble learning to use it. I don't even know if we're getting trained. Thankfully, the community college offers tutorials in Page Creator. I'm glad we won't be using it for another six months.*

7. What is the problem?

8. What are some ways you could address the problem? What are potential consequences of each?

Summary ■ ■ ■

Employees who are good learners apply their existing knowledge and skills. To be a good learner, make sure you are doing the following:

- **Employing learning strategies** Do not try to master something new all at once. Practice and focus on one new skill at a time.

- **Applying knowledge and skills** Share your knowledge and skills with others—teaching another person is a great way to reinforce what you know.

- **Participating in training** Always participate in training, even if you do not see an immediate need for it. Doing so helps you be prepared for any changes.

- **Anticipating changes in work** Try to envision how any expected changes will affect your work. Have a plan for getting through the "learning curve" period.

Answers begin on page 135.

Lesson 16 ■ ■ ■
Understanding Business

In any industry, the most valuable employees are those who are capable of seeing the big picture. They consider how their actions affect the rest of the team, and they keep up with new developments in their field. Employees who understand business monitor work situations and try to understand them in context. They also have an understanding of business ethics and market trends.

Skill Examples ■ ■

Situational Awareness Alexander and Lucille both hold entry-level positions at their respective companies. Both have been assigned tasks and have had trouble completing them.

Read the two examples and answer the questions that follow.

EXAMPLE 1 **Alexander's Inventory**

> Alexander works as a distribution receiver at a warehouse for electronics. His supervisor, Joe, asks him to complete an inventory and to give it to Lily, who is in charge of ordering supplies. She uses the inventory to help her make decisions about quantities. Alexander has little experience and interest in doing inventories and is unable to complete the count accurately. He does not understand that any errors will impact ordering, sales, and revenue. The following month, the warehouse is oversupplied with MP3 players and has too few popular cell phones.

1. Based on Alexander's actions, why might Joe perceive that he is not knowledgeable about business?
   A. Alexander provides an accurate count of the items in the warehouse.
   B. Alexander completes the inventory without any concern for accuracy.
   C. Alexander does not complete the inventory quickly enough.
   D. Alexander does not give the inventory to Lily.
   E. Alexander does not like doing inventories.

2. What might have happened if Alexander had been aware of the impact his work would have on others?
   F. He might have quit his job.
   G. He might have told Joe that completing an inventory was too menial a task for him.
   H. He might have made sure to complete the count accurately or notified someone about his difficulties.
   J. He might have told his coworkers to learn to do inventories.
   K. He might have realized that none of the products are selling well.

Remember!
Understand Systems
Part of understanding systems is knowing how your work can impact others and the company's success. In *Example 1*, Alexander is unaware that mistakes in an inventory can affect ordering, revenue, and sales. As a result of Alexander's inaccurate inventory, Lily orders too many MP3 players and not enough cell phones. This negatively affects the company's profits and reputation, since its stores will be unable to meet customers' demands.

EXAMPLE 2 Lucille's Camera Malfunction

Lucille has a job as a technology assistant for a private security firm. She performs tasks related to installing, monitoring, and repairing security equipment. One day, she notices that a video camera is not functioning properly. The video is repeatedly interrupted by static. Lucille decides to notify her boss that the camera is malfunctioning and may need to be replaced. She knows that there are twelve similar cameras elsewhere on the premises. Lucille checks each of these cameras in case there is a global issue. She then contacts her boss to say that three of the video cameras are malfunctioning.

3. How do Lucille's actions show that she is an alert, aware employee?
   A. She tries to handle most equipment repairs by herself.
   B. She realizes that a minor malfunction may be a sign of a larger problem.
   C. She continually updates her boss about how the situation is developing.
   D. She knows about all of the latest trends in high-tech security equipment.
   E. She assumes that all the other video cameras are working.

4. What would most likely have happened if Lucille had not checked all twelve video cameras?
   F. Lucille would not have needed to report the problem to her boss.
   G. All of the cameras in the building would have functioned perfectly.
   H. The problem with the video would have resolved itself in time.
   J. She and her boss would not have known the extent of the problem.
   K. Her boss would have decided to contact the camera's manufacturer.

Think About It Think about how Alexander and Lucille encountered problems at work. What level of awareness did each employee display? How did each employee seek out additional information that might be useful? Which one of them is likely to be more successful in his or her line of work? In forming your answer, think about the following questions:

- **Solve Problems** Alexander and Lucille each had to address a problematic situation. How did they solve their problems?

- **Use Systems** How aware were Alexander and Lucille about where their particular tasks fit within the larger company and how their work might impact others?

Remember!
Monitor and Correct Performance

Situational awareness involves anticipating potential problems and taking precautions. In *Example 2*, Lucille does not assume that only one video camera is malfunctioning. She reasons that it is worth her time to check all twelve cameras for the same problem. By doing so, she finds other malfunctioning cameras and is able to provide her boss with a complete report on the problem. This saves time since she does not have to report the same problem repeatedly. It also demonstrates to her boss that she is responsible and takes initiative.

Try It Out! ■ ■ ■

Market Knowledge Mel is an assistant at a botanical nursery that gets much of its business from local florists. He subscribes to a trade journal about trends in gardening and floral design. One morning, he reads the following tip.

> Big, bold, and beautiful—that's the trend for wedding flowers this spring! If there's one flower that's at the top of everyone's list, it's hydrangeas. These lush blooms are gorgeous in everything from bridal bouquets to table centerpieces. Lavender, pink, and blue are the "in" colors for spring, but this versatile flower is available in a wide range of colors. Stock up now!

Mel knows that the nursery's owner is not overly fond of hydrangeas. In fact, the nursery has relatively few hydrangea bushes. However, based on the article, Mel thinks it might be wise to have more hydrangeas in stock. Mel wants the nursery to take advantage of trends, but he does not want to overstep his boundaries as an employee. He is not sure what he should do.

Decision-Making Process				
STEP 1: Identify the Problem	**STEP 2:** Locate, Gather, and Organize Relevant Information	**STEP 3:** Generate Alternatives	**STEP 4:** Choose a Solution	**STEP 5:** Implement the Solution
Mel wants to take advantage of a possible trend, but he does not want to overstep his boundaries.	The nursery gets business from local florists. A trade journal says hydrangeas will be popular this spring. Mel's boss dislikes hydrangeas and keeps few in stock.	Mel can immediately tell his boss he should get more hydrangea plants. Mel can do additional research on this trend and report his findings to his boss.	Mel wants to take advantage of a possible market trend. However, he does not want to undermine his boss's authority. He chooses to do additional research and then share his findings with his boss.	Mel does additional research that supports what he learned. Mel shares his findings with his boss.

Mel's first option is to tell his boss to order more hydrangea plants. However, he realizes that he cannot make a strong case based on one article. His boss might ignore Mel's recommendation if it is based on one person's opinion. Mel decides he should explore this possible trend further. He finds that many trade journals predict the same trend—that hydrangeas will be popular in spring. Even their competitors mention on their websites that they will have a variety of hydrangea plants in spring. Mel shows his boss the information and shares the prediction with him. His boss then acts on the information.

Remember!

Know How to Learn
You can become a more knowledgeable and valuable employee by educating yourself about industry trends. Keep up with what competitors are doing. Reading about your field, attending industry events, and talking with other professionals are all good ways to stay informed. By keeping informed, Mel spots a trend early enough to share it with his boss and thus benefit the business.

Market Knowledge For several years, Chloe has worked as a hostess at a Mexican restaurant. She has noticed that certain times of year tend to be especially busy. The busiest period of all is early May when many people celebrate Cinco de Mayo. The week before the holiday, Chloe overhears a newly hired manager placing a food order.

> *We need to restock the following items: corn and flour tortillas, chicken, beef, tomatoes, limes, and jalapeño peppers. Actually, I'm new here and I'm not sure about the quantities. Just supply the usual amount of each item and that should be fine. Thank you.*

Chloe is worried that the new manager is not making an informed decision. The restaurant is very popular in the community. Many customers dine there during the week of Cinco de Mayo. Chloe thinks they should probably order more food than usual. However, she does not want to tell the manager how to do his job, so she decides to say nothing.

1. Which of the following is a potential consequence of Chloe's decision?
   A. The restaurant will be able to keep its regular customers happy.
   B. The restaurant will run out of some food items next week.
   C. The manager will decide to close the restaurant on Cinco de Mayo.
   D. The manager will not educate himself about the restaurant's busy periods.
   E. The restaurant supplier will know to send more food because Cinco de Mayo is approaching.

2. How should Chloe have handled the situation differently to ensure the restaurant would run smoothly?
   F. She should have asked to be scheduled for additional shifts next week.
   G. She should have contacted the supplier on her own and ordered more food.
   H. She should have told the restaurant owner that the new manager seems very unprepared for his job.
   J. She should have told the manager to swap duties with her.
   K. She should have informed the manager that he may need to order additional supplies to handle the increased business.

Reflect In both of the *Try It Out!* examples, the employees carefully observed trends in their industries. They both made decisions about how to use their market knowledge and their awareness of industry trends and whether or not to communicate with supervisory staff. Do you think each employee made the correct decision? What effect might their decisions have on business? How might the outcome of each situation have changed based on a different set of actions?

Remember!

Acquire and Use Information Make an effort to obtain information and use it to the benefit of your coworkers and the company. You can acquire information by conducting your own research or by communicating with your coworkers. Having the right information can help you make informed decisions to get the job done well. For example, the manager of the restaurant where Chloe works could have consulted with staff before ordering supplies. This would have helped avoid a mistake that could cost the company money and customers.

On Your Own ■ ■ ■

Read the following scenarios. Then answer the questions that follow each scenario.

SCENARIO A Situational Awareness

As an electrician, you are working with a construction team to build a house.

> Today you are scheduled to finish putting in the wiring in the master bedroom. After you complete this task, the team will begin installing drywall there. However, you have a bad cold and are not feeling well. You would like to go home early and rest. If you do so, the wiring will not be completed today.

Complete the chart below and then answer the questions that follow.

Decision-Making Process				
STEP 1: Identify the Problem	**STEP 2:** Locate, Gather, and Organize Relevant Information	**STEP 3:** Generate Alternatives	**STEP 4:** Choose a Solution	**STEP 5:** Implement the Solution
You are scheduled to finish the wiring, but you want to leave early because you are sick.	You cannot complete the wiring if you go home early. Drywall cannot be installed until the wiring is finished.			

1. What solution did you choose to implement for this problem?

2. To whom, if anyone, would you need to communicate your solution?

SCENARIO B Business Ethics

You work as a pharmaceutical salesperson. You and some coworkers are attending an out-of-state conference in a large city. You hope to enjoy the nightlife while you are away. A coworker, Janelle, discusses possible evening plans with you.

> *Those seminars today were so dull! I can't wait to relax and unwind. I know some people are heading out to dinner with all the senior managers, but that sounds boring. A couple of us are planning to check out the dance club on Eighth Street. I know it doesn't have a great reputation, but after a day like today, I am ready to dance! Do you want to come?*

You are unsure of how to respond to Janelle. Since several of your top clients are also in attendance at the conference, they are likely to be at the same places as you are.

3. What are some of your alternatives for how to respond to your coworker's invitation? What are the potential consequences of choosing each alternative?

4. What choice is the most appropriate for this situation? Why?

SCENARIO C Market Knowledge

In your duties as a graphic designer, you often develop logos for small businesses. The owner of a sporting goods store approaches you about creating a logo.

> The store owner has strong opinions about how he wants the logo to look. He would like to incorporate images of athletic gear, such as tennis rackets and sneakers. You suspect that this idea is dated. You research current trends and competitors' logos. This research confirms your suspicions, and you believe that a simple, typographic logo would be the best choice for his business.

5. What is the problem you must solve?

6. What are some ways you could solve this problem?

7. Which solution would show that you understand your client's needs?

SCENARIO D Business Ethics

As an interior designer, you have been hired by a wealthy client to design a bathroom. You are working together to identify and purchase materials.

> Your company offers several high-end, expensive options for lighting, tiles, and fixtures. You would like to recommend these items. Doing so would net your materials supplier, who is a close friend, a greater profit on this job. You know your client can easily afford top-of-the-line materials. Still, your client's tastes are fairly simple. You think she would probably be equally satisfied with your less expensive options. However, this would result in your friend making less money from the job. You are not sure which options you should present to the client.

8. What information is available to help you make a decision?

9. What actions might you take and what might their consequences be?

Summary ▪ ▪ ▪

Employees who understand business understand their place within a business. To ensure that you are business-savvy, keep the following points in mind:

- **Situational awareness** Identify your workplace's "big picture." Try to understand your tasks in the context of the business as a whole.

- **Business ethics** Maintain high ethical standards—even if doing so occasionally conflicts with your short-term preferences. In the long run, displaying sound ethics will enhance your reputation and make you more successful.

- **Market knowledge** Stay informed about trends, innovations, and best practices in your industry.

Answers begin on page 136.

Job Seeker's Toolkit

The *Job Seeker's Toolkit* is a valuable resource that will help guide you through the job search process. It is full of useful tips and examples. The *Toolkit* will help you identify career options and discover ways to search and apply for jobs. It also provides tips for interviewing and following up after an interview.

Step 1: Explore Careers

See pages 110–111.

Recognize Strengths and Opportunities One of the first actions you need to take in planning a career is to identify your skills. Knowing your strengths and weaknesses will help you match your skills to a suitable job. This includes determining your abilities, skills, preferences, and interests. You also need to identify opportunities by finding fast-growing fields or in-demand careers. Online job sites and newspaper classified ads can help you discover who is hiring and which professions are in demand.

Create a Personal Fact Sheet Making a comprehensive list of your past is one of the most practical things you can do in your job hunt. Putting everything in one document will help you pick the most appropriate items to include in your résumé. In addition, having this document with you when applying for jobs will ensure that you complete your applications quickly and accurately.

See page 112.

Seek Out Additional Education and Training When considering a new job or career, you will need to find out if additional training, experience, or education is required. Taking educational courses or practical training can greatly increase your attractiveness to employers. You must also keep abreast of developments in your areas of interest. Being up to date in your field demonstrates your interest in the subject and an eagerness to learn.

Step 2: Search for Jobs

See pages 113–114.

Network Recognize the power of networking in finding and getting a job. Although searching online may help you find a job, many job openings are not publicly advertised. Your best shot at finding these jobs is to build your network of friends and acquaintances—both online and offline. People in your network can serve as references and provide letters of recommendation.

Create an Online Profile An online profile displays your skills and work experience for colleagues and potential employers to see. It is also a way to connect professionally with others and build your network.

See pages 115–116.

Find Job Opportunities Searching online is probably the fastest, easiest, and cheapest way to look for a job. Other good resources include newspaper classified ads, career fairs, temp agencies, and job-search firms. Learning how to tailor your search to find the jobs you want will save you time and make your job search more focused.

Step 3: Apply for Jobs

Create a Résumé Your résumé is often the first exposure a prospective employer has to you. It is therefore vital that both the style and the content of your résumé make you look as impressive as possible. A résumé gives your prospective employer a record of your qualifications, experience, and skills. It can also tell an employer other things about you, such as your attention to detail, your command of language, and your level of creativity.

Write a Cover Letter Along with your résumé, your cover letter creates a first impression of you. Again, both style and content are important. You need to present information that will convince prospective employers to interview you. You also must write clearly, accurately, and persuasively.

Fill Out a Job Application You may have to fill out an application for a position even if you have submitted a cover letter and a résumé. The application may be on paper or online. This document serves as a record of your personal and professional history. Take the time and effort to make sure it is error-free, accurate, and complete.

Step 4: Interview for Jobs

Use Interview Etiquette Once you have a job interview, you must use that opportunity to promote yourself and get the job. There are several things job seekers should be aware of before they attend an interview.

See pages 117–118.

Answer and Ask Questions Effectively A job interview is not only about answering the interviewer's questions. It is also your opportunity to ask questions about the job and the company. Being prepared for these questions and answers can be the difference between a good interview and a bad one.

See pages 119–120.

Step 5: Follow Up

Write a Thank You Letter After a job interview, be sure to write a thank you letter to the interviewer in a professionally appropriate manner. Even if you are no longer interested in the position, it is important to thank the interviewer for his or her time.

Evaluate and Accept an Offer When you receive a job offer, you must carefully assess it and decide whether to accept it or not. You may want to negotiate the salary and benefits first. Regardless of your decision, you must convey your choice clearly, politely, and professionally.

See page 121.

Write a Follow-up Letter The most professional way to respond to a job offer or rejection is to write a follow-up letter. You should also write a letter if you decide to withdraw your application from consideration at any point during the process.

For more information and practice with the skills needed to recognize strengths and opportunities, see:

**Lesson 2:
Getting Organized**

**Lesson 15:
Being a Good Learner**

Tech Tips!

Career interest inventories and self-assessment tools can help you learn more about your strengths, personality, and values. You can research self-assessment tools—such as questionnaires, surveys, and tests—online to help you with your career planning.

Explore Careers ...

Recognize Strengths and Opportunities

You may have no idea what you want to do for a career, or you may have several ideas and not know how to choose. You need to think about which careers have available jobs. Most importantly, however, you need to find a career and job that are right for you. You can make the process easier by identifying your interests and strengths and then finding opportunities that match your skill set.

Interests and Preferences

Questions such as these help you think about your interests and preferences. Record others that are not in this list, and then answer each question.

- Do you like to work indoors or outdoors?
- Do you like to be physically active and on your feet?
- Do you like deskwork? Paperwork?
- Do you like working with customers?
- Do you enjoy working with children? The elderly?
- Do you like caring for animals or plants?
- Are you interested in health and medicine?
- Do you like being creative?

Skills and Abilities

Answer these questions to help you think about your skills and abilities. List other strengths that are not included.

- Are you good at organizing information? Keeping records?
- Are you a good listener? Are you supportive?
- Are you good at math and computations?
- Are you a good writer? Are you artistic?
- Can you speak other languages?
- Are you scientific?
- Are you good at giving advice or explaining? Are you tactful?
- Are you good at selling an idea or object?
- Are you mechanical? Can you repair things?
- Can you use computers or other equipment?

Planning Your Career ▪ ▪ ▪

Now use what you have learned about your interests, preferences, skills, and abilities to find a career that is right for you. Follow these steps to create a career plan.

Step 1: Review Your Findings Review your answers to the questions to identify your interests and strengths.

Step 2: Identify Career Clusters Find career clusters that match your interests and strengths. For example, if you are interested in nature, enjoy working outside, and have an ability to grow things, you might want to explore a career related to Agriculture, Food & Natural Resources. Other career clusters include Finance, Education & Training, Health Science, and Information Technology.

Step 3: Research Clusters and Specific Jobs Once you have identified career clusters that match your interests and strengths, research those clusters and the jobs within them that interest you most. There are several ways to research careers:

- **Online and Print Resources** Go online or to your local library to learn about the nature of general industries, working conditions, average earnings, and job outlooks. The Bureau of Labor Statistics updates its *Occupational Outlook Handbook* every two years and is available online and in print. This handbook provides detailed information on thousands of careers and occupations.

- **Hands-On Experience** Get real-world experience by shadowing someone in a field of interest. For example, if you are interested in working with the elderly, you might want to spend several days following a nurse's aide or social worker at a nursing home. You can also apply for an internship or serve as a volunteer in your field of interest.

- **Interview** If you know someone working in a field that may interest you, ask him or her for an informational interview either in person or by phone. Before the interview, research the career or field and prepare questions to ask.

Step 4: Identify Qualifications Find out what qualifications are needed for the jobs that interest you. Do these match your skills? Are there any skills you need to improve or obtain?

Step 5: Create an Improvement Plan Identify areas that need improvement, and develop a plan for gaining these skills. In addition to figuring out how you are going to gain these skills, create a time line for obtaining them.

Seek Out Additional Education and Training ▪ ▪ ▪

For more information and practice with skills needed to seek out additional education and training, see:

Lesson 15: Being a Good Learner

You may need additional education or training to qualify for certain jobs or to advance beyond an entry-level position. Perhaps you need to improve in areas where you struggle, or acquire specific skills, or even finish a degree.

There are several ways to obtain the necessary training and education for a wide variety of careers. Start by looking for resources in your own community.

Community Centers Community centers often post jobs, trainings, courses, or workshops on a bulletin board or in a local publication. These opportunities are convenient and affordable for people who live in the community.

Community Colleges Community colleges offer a variety of classes across industries and disciplines. Community colleges also staff academic advisors and enrollment counselors who advise students about education and career decisions.

Colleges and Universities Nearby institutions not only offer courses but also host academic and professional activities year-round. They attract job fairs and other large-scale events that allow members of the community to participate.

Vocational and Trade Schools Vocational and trade schools are designed to teach skills specifically needed for particular careers. These schools provide targeted focus for individuals who already know what job, trade, or skill they are interested in. These programs are often short-term and affordable.

Military The military provides specific and intense training for individuals who enlist (who agree to join for at least four years). The military is a major commitment, and many risks need to be considered. However, the rewards of the commitment and training provide benefits for a lifetime.

If the right educational opportunities are not available in your community, consider the virtual classroom. Many colleges and universities offer online courses that can be accessed through the Internet.

On-the-Job Training ▪ ▪ ▪

Some employers offer formal on-the-job training. These programs allow you to learn the necessary skills while at work, instead of requiring you to have mastered the skills before being hired.

Apprenticeships Apprenticeships allow aspiring tradespersons to learn a trade directly from an expert. Apprentices are often compensated for their time and are able to network once in the community of the trade.

Internships Internships also allow aspiring workers to gain experience in a specific field. Internships are offered for a short amount of time, but once inside a company, interns can often advance quickly.

Keep in mind that whatever education, experience, or training you seek, the basic skills you develop will benefit all jobs and industries. Critical thinking, reading, writing, and basic mathematics are necessary skills in all careers.

Tech Tips!

If you do not have access to the Internet at home, go to your local library. Many libraries offer free use of computers and Internet access. Use the library's online resources to search for jobs, internships, apprenticeships, and classes in your area. The librarians are also willing to help you locate and navigate online career and employment information.

Search for Jobs ...

Network ...

Networking is an effective tool to use when looking for a job. When you talk to friends, family, and acquaintances about potential jobs, you are participating in networking. People you know can often put you in contact with specific individuals within a company. These individuals can tell you about job openings or guide you to other people who may be helpful. When you apply for these jobs, you can use your contacts as references.

List Existing Contacts ...

To start networking, create a list of contacts. This list will help you see how many people in your life are available to help you.

Family and Friends Start with your family and friends. These individuals should be people close to you with whom you could speak openly about your job search and goals. They should be individuals who care about your success and will be enthusiastic about helping you.

Educational and Professional Contacts Think about people you know from your current and prior workplaces and from volunteer work. Also list instructors and fellow students from school, workshops, and training programs. Put an asterisk next to those who have been especially supportive or helpful.

Make New Contacts ...

It is important to identify your known contacts, but keep in mind that networking can happen through acquaintances and even chance interactions. Be open to expanding your circle by networking at social events or while doing day-to-day activities. You may meet a new neighbor at a barbecue, a fellow pet lover at the veterinarian, or a business owner at the dry cleaner. Each of these individuals may lead to a networking opportunity.

Also, be on the lookout for networking events at universities, organizations, associations, and businesses. Some events are free, while others require a small fee. Once you meet a few people, ask them if they know anyone else at the event. Although the event is designed for finding professional connections, talk about your other interests to help forge a personal connection and to show your unique personality.

CONSIDER ALL YOUR POSSIBLE CONTACTS

- Family and friends
- Neighbors
- Classmates
- Acquaintances
- Instructors/Teachers
- Organization/Club members
- Current and former coworkers
- Current and former employers

For more information and practice with skills needed to network, see:

**Lesson 2:
Getting Organized**

**Lesson 5:
Interacting with Others**

Tech Tips!

Be aware of your online presence while networking. If you belong to social or professional networking sites, evaluate your profile(s) before contacting others about possible opportunities. Many employers turn to the Internet to investigate potential new hires.

Talk to Contacts ▪ ▪ ▪

Once you have a list of existing contacts, you are ready to network. That is, you are ready to let your contacts know that you are looking for work. Whether you talk in person, by e-mail, or on the phone, keep in mind your goals for the conversation.

Get in Touch Networking does not always require a meeting in person. Use a variety of communication tools to get in touch with your contacts: telephone, e-mail, or even instant messaging. Talk to as many contacts as you can, but be respectful of their time and schedules.

Ask Open-Ended Questions Questions that require more than a yes or no answer successfully start a discussion and keep it going. You will also learn a lot more about a particular business, employer, job, or industry.

Be Yourself Be honest about your goals and experience. An open, genuine conversation will produce the best results.

Be Ready to Talk about Yourself Your contacts will also seek information from you. They will likely want to know what work you are interested in, where you have worked in the past, and how you want to improve or change your career.

Make Connections ▪ ▪ ▪

After talking to your contacts or meeting new people, you may have gathered a few names, e-mail addresses, or phone numbers of potential employers. What should you do with this information?

Stay Organized Keep track of the information you receive from your contacts. You may need to refer to names, dates, and locations when reaching out to a potential new employer.

Remain Professional Although you may have spoken to a personal contact, the connection you make will ultimately be professional. Remain professional during all correspondences, especially the first time you reach out. Consider whether an e-mail, a telephone call, or a meeting would be most appropriate for introducing yourself.

Establish a Connection Be sure to mention the name of your contact. For example, in an e-mail to a human resources manager, you could explain, "I was given your e-mail address by Rachel Marshall, my sister-in-law, who works in the accounting department."

Follow Up After a successful conversation, follow up with your contact. Let him or her know how you used the information, and remember to express your appreciation.

Be a Contact Yourself You can also network for others. It is likely that you can provide contacts for a friend or family member who is looking for a job.

Find Job Opportunities ...

Searching for job opportunities can seem overwhelming, but there are strategies and resources that can make your search easier and more successful. These include online searches, job fairs, print advertisements, cold calls, employment agencies, and temporary staffing firms.

Online Job Searches ...

One of the most popular ways to look for job opportunities is online. By searching online, you have the ability to check thousands of job postings.

JOB-SEARCH TIPS

- Find job sites that contain postings in your field of interest.

- Verify that the posting is not a scam. A posting that promises $60,000 for working at home is probably not legitimate.

- Post your résumé so employers can find and contact you.

- Create an online profile. Use it to identify your interests, skills, or salary requirements.

- Sign up for e-mail alerts when new postings in your area of interest are created.

- Use an advanced search option to narrow the results of your search. For example, instead of searching for administrative assistant jobs, you can search for administrative assistant jobs that are available in your city in a particular industry.

Job Fairs ...

Job fairs are a great way for employers and job seekers to meet. At job fairs, employers set up tables or booths, discuss job opportunities with attendees, collect résumés, and hand out business cards.

BEFORE ATTENDING A JOB FAIR, DO THE FOLLOWING

- Research which companies are participating. Identify the companies that you are interested in.

- List questions to ask company representatives, such as "What is the growth potential at your company?"

- Practice answering interview questions. You may get interviewed on the spot.

- Prepare a brief introduction. When you introduce yourself, you want to sound like you know what you are looking for. Avoid sounding too rehearsed.

ON THE DAY OF THE JOB FAIR, REMEMBER TO

- Dress neatly and professionally.

- Take copies of your résumé to hand out. Make sure all the information is up to date.

- Take a folder, a notebook, and a pen. Use the folder to hold copies of your résumé. Use the notebook to take notes of your conversations.

For more information and practice with the skills needed to be successful while searching for job opportunities, see:

**Lesson 2:
Getting Organized**

**Lesson 13:
Being Self-Motivated**

Tech Tips!

When posting a résumé or similar information online, be sure to check the privacy settings on the site. For your protection, some websites may block portions of your information from public view, but others will not. This means that your name, address, and telephone number could be made public.

Print Advertisements ▪ ▪ ▪

You can also find job advertisements in newspapers and magazines. These ads are typically short, containing the job title, required skills, tasks, location, and contact information. Keep in mind that you should not depend entirely on print ads. Only a small number of people find jobs using this search method.

Cold Calls ▪ ▪ ▪

Cold calls are telephone calls or e-mail messages inquiring about job openings. They are made without prior contact and are not in response to a job ad.

BEFORE YOU BEGIN COLD CALLING

- Make a list of companies you are interested in contacting. To do this, consider where you would like to work.

- Write a brief introduction that explains who you are, why you are contacting the company, and your qualifications.

- Create a list of questions.

IF YOU DECIDE TO MAKE THE COLD CALL VIA TELEPHONE

- Ask for the Human Resources or Personnel Manager. Once you are connected, introduce yourself and ask if the company has any open positions.

- Be sure to repeat important information and thank your contact at the end of the call.

- Be polite.

IF YOU DECIDE TO MAKE THE COLD CALL VIA E-MAIL

- Have a clear, interesting subject line. Make sure it does not appear to be spam mail.

- Personalize your message. Do not send the same standard e-mail to a dozen companies.

- Be concise. The employer may have dozens (if not hundreds) of e-mails to read. If your message is long, it may not get read.

- Include your résumé with your message.

Employment Agencies and Temporary Staffing Firms (or Temp Agencies) ▪ ▪ ▪

An employment agency helps match job seekers with employers. Companies contact the agency when they have job openings. If the employer is looking for someone with your qualifications, the agency will bring you and the company together.

A temp agency helps connect workers with employers who are in need of additional staff members for a specific period of time. Temp agencies allow workers to gain experience and learn about various occupations.

Interview for Jobs ...
Use Interview Etiquette ...

After reviewing your cover letter and résumé, employers may contact you for the next stage of the hiring process: the interview. Your résumé and cover letter provide employers with a general sense of your qualifications for the job. The interview provides them with an opportunity to get more specific information and to follow up on information provided in your résumé and cover letter.

While each interview and interviewer are different, there are some basic rules that can be applied to most interviews.

Before the Interview ...

Planning ahead and being prepared can help reduce your stress and enable you to perform to the best of your ability during the interview.

Know Where You Are Going Confirm the date, time, and place of the interview. If you are not familiar with the location, get detailed directions in advance. You can find the address and directions online.

Know Who You Are Meeting Know the name and job title of the individual you will be meeting with. If you are unsure of the individual's title or how to pronounce his or her name, call the company to confirm the information or research it on the company's website. Often interviews are scheduled by Human Resources (HR) personnel. You may be met by an HR representative who will then introduce you to your interviewer.

Be Prepared Prepare everything you will need for your interview the night before. Make sure you select what clothes you will wear, plan how to get to the interview, and have everything you may need at the interview. There are a few items that you should always bring, such as copies of your résumé, the job posting, and any official documents you may need. (You should bring hard copies of these documents even if you have already sent electronic versions.) You should also bring any items that the interviewer specifically requested. Use the checklist below as a guide when you prepare for an interview.

INTERVIEW CHECKLIST ☑

- ☐ Personal fact sheet
- ☐ Copies of your résumé
- ☐ List of questions you want to ask
- ☐ Work permit or work visa (if any)
- ☐ State-issued ID
- ☐ Social Security card

- ☐ Pens and a notebook
- ☐ Copy of the job posting
- ☐ Name, title, phone number, and e-mail address of interviewer contact
- ☐ Any materials requested by the interviewer

For more information and practice with the skills needed to be successful on an interview, see:

Lesson 1: Dependability and Reliability

Lesson 5: Interacting with Others

Lesson 6: Active Listening

Lesson 7: Effective Speaking

Tech Tips!

Researching a company before you interview is a great way to make sure you are prepared. Most companies have websites where you can find most of the information you are looking for. You can use the company's website to find the company's address and directions to the interview location. The website may also contain an online directory, which you can use to make sure your contact information is correct.

At the Interview ▪ ▪ ▪

On the day of the interview it is important to dress and behave appropriately in order to make the best impression possible. There are some simple rules that you can follow to ensure that your interview goes well.

Behave Professionally Make sure you are professionally dressed. Your clothes should be clean and pressed. Avoid heavy jewelry, makeup, and perfume.

Arrive for your interview early. This will allow you to complete any required paperwork. It also will show that you are dependable and reliable and that you respect the interviewer's time. Turn off your cell phone so you can give the interviewer your undivided attention. Introduce yourself and shake hands. When introduced to others, smile and shake hands.

Demonstrate Good Speaking and Listening Skills During the interview it is important to display good speaking and listening skills. Speak clearly and confidently and avoid slang. It is okay to take a little time to think about a question before answering. Sit or stand straight, and look the interviewer in the eye. Avoid fidgeting, slouching, or looking down.

When the interviewer is speaking, listen carefully without interrupting, and pay close attention for important information. Take notes on anything you want to remember or ask about later. Maintain eye contact and nod, or use other nonverbal cues to indicate that you are paying attention and understand.

INTERVIEW TIPS

At the interview, remember to:

- Speak loudly, clearly, and confidently.

- Be precise. Provide an answer to the question asked.

- Be honest. Do not just tell the interviewer what you think he or she wants to hear.

- Pay attention to what your interviewer says. Ask for clarification if you need it.

- Avoid speaking badly about your past employers.

After the Interview ▪ ▪ ▪

Thank your interviewer for his or her time and for the opportunity. Before leaving, ask the interviewer what you might expect moving forward and when you will be contacted next. Follow up with the interviewer by sending a brief thank you e-mail or letter.

TIPS FOR FOLLOWING UP

- Make sure you are aware of the next steps that need to be taken.

- Send thank you notes to each person you met with.

- Contact your interviewer if you have not heard from him or her on the agreed-upon date. Ask for an update, and express your continued interest in the position.

Answer and Ask Questions Effectively ▪ ▪

During a job interview, you expect to answer questions about your interests, experience, education, and qualifications. You must also be prepared to ask your own questions about the business and the position. Anticipating how to answer and ask these questions effectively can inspire confidence, reduce stress, and ensure a good experience.

Answer Questions ▪ ▪

Although companies and businesses can be unique in their operations and hiring practices, most ask the same kinds of questions in an interview. You can expect to answer questions about your interests, work experience, and ethics.

Questions about Your Interests Interviewers typically open the conversation with questions about your personal interests and activities. The interviewer may ask questions like the following:

- What do you like to do in your free time?

- What are your strengths and weaknesses?

- What is one accomplishment that you are proud of? Why?

- Where do you see yourself in five years?

You can prepare to answer these questions by thinking about your responses beforehand. Write down your ideas and bring them to the interview. Answer genuinely, but be sure to connect your answers to the job or company.

Questions about Your Work Experience Interviewers have selected you for an interview because they were impressed by your résumé and cover letter. However, your résumé shows only a snapshot of your work experience. Expect to answer questions based on the details of your résumé. For example, you may be asked to clarify duties from a previous position. Bring at least one copy of your résumé to the interview so you can consult it when answering questions. Use it as a guide or a place to start as you answer and add more specifics.

Questions about Your Ethics Some questions may require you to use critical thinking skills. For example, an interviewer may present a job-related scenario. Oftentimes these scenarios contain an ethical component. The interviewer wants to see whether you can solve problems and support the company's ethics. There are no right answers to these kinds of questions. Be resourceful and creative with your response, and you will make a positive impression.

Questions Unrelated to Work What happens when an interviewer asks a question unrelated to work? Certain laws do not allow employers to ask about your age, race, citizenship, or marital status. You are not obligated to answer these questions. So, how can you steer the conversation back to a relevant topic? An effective response will acknowledge the question but return to your qualifications.

For more information and practice with skills needed to ask and answer questions effectively, see:

Lesson 3:
Verifying Information

Lesson 6:
Active Listening

Lesson 7:
Effective Speaking

Ask Your Own Questions ▪ ▪ ▪

Asking your own good questions shows you are genuinely interested in the company and the position. Prepare questions before the interview. You will usually get a chance to ask them after the interviewer has asked his or her questions. Start with the following and include some of your own.

- What do employees in other positions do?
- Is it possible to advance and earn promotions?
- What opportunities are there for growth and development?
- Are employee benefits available?
- Will I need to relocate or travel at any time?

Using Nonverbal Communication ▪ ▪ ▪

Answering and asking questions is not always about what you say. It is also about how you present yourself.

Before the interview, generate questions and responses. Then, in front of a mirror, watch yourself as you answer and ask the questions. Pay attention to your body language and facial expressions. Practice the following nonverbal communication skills to ensure positive body language while asking and answering questions.

- Smile.
- Maintain eye contact.
- Sit straight, but stay relaxed.
- Nod your head to show that you understand.
- Avoid motions that might distract the interviewer. (If you tend to tap your fingers or twirl your hair when you are nervous, hold a pen during the interview.)
- Dress in comfortable, appropriate clothing.

You can even ask a family member or friend to play the role of the interviewer. At the end of the role-play, ask for feedback on your verbal and nonverbal communication. Write down the feedback, and apply it as you continue to practice.

> ### TIPS FOR ANSWERING AND ASKING QUESTIONS
>
> Remember that an interview is essentially a conversation. Practice the following tips to make sure the conversation is smooth, uninterrupted, and productive.
>
> - Speak clearly and at an appropriate speed and volume.
> - Use only standard English. Avoid slang and swear words.
> - Ask for clarification if you do not understand a question.
> - Pay attention and listen carefully. Be careful not to interrupt.

Tech Tips!

Go online and review the company's website before an interview. Doing so will help you generate questions to ask. You will also impress the interviewer by being knowledgeable about the company. Consider also using a search engine to find reviews of the company's business, services, or goods.

Follow Up ...

Evaluate and Accept an Offer ...

If a company thinks you will be a good match for its needs, you will probably receive a job offer. It is important to take time to consider the offer and think about the job. Changing your mind after you have accepted the job could damage your relationship with the company and your professional reputation in general.

Job Offer Considerations

Before making a decision to accept or decline the offer, there are many issues you should consider.

Job Think about the job itself. If you will not enjoy the day-to-day work, you should not accept the offer.

Company Consider what you know about the company from your research and the interview to figure out whether the job is a good fit for you. For example, is the company new or established? Established companies may be more stable; however, helping to build a new company can be rewarding and exciting.

Salary Check that the salary matches the amount that has been agreed upon or that was posted. Make sure it is sufficient to pay your bills. Also, consider whether the salary is fair. To do this, research similar jobs in your area. If the salary is not what you want, find out whether it is possible to negotiate.

Benefits Take into account the benefits that come with the job. For example, how many sick and vacation days will you receive, what type of health and life insurance is available, and will you get paid or compensated for working overtime? Look at the salary, benefits, and any other perks as one package. For example, knowing that you have the option to work at home from time to time may add to the overall attractiveness of the offer.

Work Hours and Travel Time Have a clear understanding of how many hours you are expected to work each week and how long it takes you to get to work. This may not seem important at first, but it can have a big effect on your quality of life. For example, sitting in rush-hour traffic for an hour twice a day can be tiring and stressful. If you have a long commute, find out if the company has flexible hours. You can often avoid sitting in traffic by traveling to work before or after rush hour.

Accepting and Declining an Offer

If you decide to accept the offer, call your contact or send a letter or e-mail acknowledging that you agree to the terms. To decline the offer, write a letter or an e-mail expressing your appreciation. Be sure to leave a good impression. You might want to work at the company in the future, or you might encounter your contact in another professional setting.

For more information and practice with the skills needed to evaluate a job offer, see:

Lesson 3: Verifying Information

Lesson 5: Interacting with Others

Tech Tips!

When researching salaries in your area, you can use online salary surveys or government publications to help you figure out whether a job offer is fair. Consult multiple resources to ensure that you have a good idea about what people in your area are earning.

Answer Key ▪ ■ ▪

Lesson 1 (pp. 6–11)

Skill Examples

1. C   2. J   3. C   4. G

Think About It

Answers should focus on Brandon's and Justine's preparations. Brandon practiced for his test, selected his clothes, and planned out his route the night before. Justine left a few of these tasks until the morning. As a result, Brandon was able to arrive on time, demonstrating responsibility, while Justine arrived late. Although Justine arrived late, she demonstrates responsibility by bringing all the requested items. Still, Justine's lateness might have a negative impact on a decision to hire her. Because Brandon demonstrated that he is dependable and reliable, he is more likely to be hired.

Try It Out!

1. A   2. J

Reflect

Answers should focus on the consequences of Carlos's and Janie's actions. Carlos made the right decision because he notified his manager of the problem and worked with him to find a solution. Because of his action, he probably impressed his manager with his concern for complying with policies. Had he not contacted his manager, he may have gotten in trouble for not following the company's dress code. Janie did not make good decisions. She should have prioritized her tasks. Had she done this she would have been able to complete the assigned task on time. By not completing the task, Janie may have jeopardized the firm's relationships with some clients. The partners may also now view her as less responsible.

On Your Own

Scenario A *Possible Answers*

Step 3: a) You could take the earlier bus. b) You could take the later bus. c) You could find a different way to get to work.

Step 4: You choose to take the earlier bus in order to arrive at work on time. This bus ensures your punctual arrival.

Step 5: You plan ahead and make the necessary changes in your schedule to catch the earlier bus and arrive on time.

1. You choose to take the earlier bus in order to arrive at work on time.

2. If you took the earlier bus, or found an alternate way to work, you would not need to contact

anyone. If you took the later bus, you would need to call or e-mail your manager and let him or her know you would be late because of the change in the bus schedule.

Scenario B *Possible Answers*

3. You need to determine whether you should go to work despite your fever or stay home until you have been fever free for 24 hours.

4. a) You could go to work, but this may result in other employees or the children getting sick. You may also be reprimanded for violating company policy. b) You could stay home until you are feeling better, which would mean you would not be paid for the time you miss.

5. You choose to stay home until you are feeling better. The policy is in place to protect the children at the day care. Ignoring the policy could have serious consequences including your being fired.

Scenario C *Possible Answers*

6. a) You could go to the game and miss work. b) You could ask your manager to rearrange your schedule so you work a different weekend. c) You could work as scheduled.

7. a) You might be reprimanded for missing work, but you would be able to attend the game. b) Your manager could rearrange your schedule, but he might think you are unreliable. c) You would show that you are dependable but miss out on seeing the game.

8. If you choose to work as scheduled, you would show that you are dependable. Trying to rearrange your work schedule so that your manager can arrange for extra staff, if needed, would also show that you are reliable.

Scenario D *Possible Answers*

9. a) You could leave and finish the job first thing tomorrow, but your manager may be angry that you did not complete the job. b) You could send the document without checking it, but there may be errors. c) You could stay late to make sure there are no errors. This would mean you would have to give up some of your personal time.

10. You choose to stay late and check that you have entered all changes.

11. Yes. Your employer would see from your actions that you honor your commitments and meet deadlines even when doing so requires extra work.

Lesson 2 (pp. 12–17)

Skill Examples
1. E   2. F   3. D   4. H

Think About It

Answers should focus on Lakesha's and Jeremy's organizational skills and their preparedness. Lakesha decided to set aside time to review her students' transcripts and files before her meetings with them. She not only made notes about the problems she wanted to discuss with each student, but she also flagged important pages in the files so she could refer to them quickly during her meetings. This helped Lakesha be prepared for her sessions with her students and reduced her stress. Jeremy, on the other hand, was disorganized and chose to rely on his memory to buy the supplies needed for his painting tasks. Without a list, he forgot about or overlooked buying the required supplies and increased his stress. He should instead develop a habit of taking notes at each job site so that he can refer to his notes when it is time to order more supplies. Based on this, Lakesha is more prepared for her job.

Try It Out!
1. B   2. K

Reflect

Answers should focus on alternate solutions Mollie and Harold could have chosen and their results. Mollie could have checked to make sure she had all of the necessary equipment before setting up. This would have helped her avoid expensive shipping charges. Harold could have called ahead to let the business owner know he would be late. Both of these actions would have produced better results.

On Your Own

Scenario A *Possible Answers*

Step 3: a) You could try to complete all the tasks on your own and hope to finish on time. b) You could put off some tasks for the next day, angering your supervisor. c) You could delegate some tasks to other members of your team.

Step 4: You assign yourself tasks that can be completed only by you. Then you divide up the remaining tasks between other team members. By doing this, you are making sure all of the tasks are assigned efficiently.

Step 5: You start working on tasks that can only be done by you and have the remaining team members start working on the remainder of the tasks.

1. a) You could work efficiently and beyond the day's business hours to complete all the tasks on the same day. b) You could ask the members of your team to help you complete all your tasks. c) You could inform your supervisor that you need more

time to complete the tasks. Then you could make sure that you and your team would work together to get the job done within that time frame.

2. a) Since you would be working on your own, you would create a plan for yourself in order to complete the job that day. b) You would communicate your solution to team members so they would know what is expected of them. c) You would communicate your solution to your supervisor and the team.

Scenario B *Possible Answers*

3. Your problem is that the customer's order was not filled correctly.

4. a) You could reorder the missing items and use the standard shipping method. b) You could rush the missing items to the business owner. c) You could provide the customer with a refund for the missing portion of his order.

5. a) The business owner may be upset that he does not have all the food he needs. b) The business owner would be pleased that he would receive the rest of the order that day. However, this would require the farm to temporarily lose one worker while he or she delivers the items. c) The farm would lose money from the sale.

Scenario C *Possible Answers*

6. Your response to your manager is insufficient because it is not specific. You do not inform your manager how far along you are in taking the inventory and what you have left to do. You also do not mention whether you have any questions or problems and when you expect to be finished. Your manager might consider your response very vague and unhelpful. She might also feel that you are uninterested in your job.

7. You could have provided your manager with a more detailed response by telling and showing her how much you have completed and how long you think it will take to finish the inventory. You could also have asked her any questions you had.

Scenario D *Possible Answers*

8. Your problem is that your e-mail box is disorganized, which makes it difficult to find information.

9. a) You could reorganize your e-mail box by creating folders based on the subject of the e-mail. b) You could reorganize your e-mail box by creating folders based on the sender. You choose to organize your e-mail box based on the subject.

10. With your new organization, it will be easier to find information about specific projects and policies. You will also be able to store important messages so they can be retrieved for reference.

Lesson 3 (pp. 18–23)

Skill Examples
1. B   2. G   3. C   4. J

Think About It
Answers should focus on Ronald's and Mary's supervisor's view of their accountability and communications skills. Both employees worked independently, so their record-keeping skills were very important to their supervisors. Mary's cleaning logs were not complete, so her supervisor could not be sure whether Mary had completed her assigned duties. Mary's supervisor might also have thought that Mary needed to improve her communications skills. Ronald regularly updated the logs as he cleaned a room. His supervisor could trust that if he declared a room clean, then it probably was. Based on this, Ronald would be more likely to be trusted with tasks that require more independence.

Try It Out!
1. A   2. F

Reflect
Answers should focus on how Joellen and Aaron took responsibility for verifying information. Joellen was not confident in her note taking, so she made the good decision to schedule another visit to remeasure the windows. Her supervisor would be pleased that Joellen corrected the information before sending it to the senior designer. To prevent the error from occurring, Joellen could have rechecked her notes when she met the client the first time. This way she would not have had to reschedule a visit. By doing so, Joellen could have efficiently given her notes to the senior designer who was in charge of preparing the sketch. This would have saved time and effort for her. Aaron realized that information on a supply form was incorrect. Because the human resources manager was not available, he made a judgment to submit the order form. Aaron's supervisor may not be happy that Aaron submitted an order he thought was incorrect. To prevent this error from happening, Aaron could have checked the order form as soon as he received it or waited to submit the order until he was able to verify that it was correct.

On Your Own
Scenario A *Possible Answers*
Step 3: a) You could drive back to the office to pick up the paperwork, which might make you late for the flight arrival. b) You could go into the airport without a sign and hope the client approaches you. c) You could contact your dispatcher and ask for the client's information.

Step 4: You choose to contact your dispatcher and ask for the client's information. This allows you to be at the pick-up point on time to receive your customer.

Step 5: You call your dispatcher and explain that you left the form at the office. The dispatcher gives you the client's name, and you write out your sign.

1. a) You could drive back to the office to pick up the paperwork. b) You could go into the airport without a sign and hope the client approaches you. c) You could contact your dispatcher and ask for the client's information.

2. You choose to call your dispatcher for the client's name and other information. Doing so allows you to pick up your customer on time. It also allows your customer to avoid an inconvenient arrival experience. However, calling your dispatcher for your client's name shows your dispatcher that you are a little careless about your work. It shows that you lack organizational skills.

Scenario B *Possible Answers*
3. The problem is that the pricing information on the order form is incorrect. You need to decide whether to recalculate the total to reflect the correct pricing or send the form as is.

4. If you forward the form as it is, the customer may pay the wrong amount for the ordered items.

Scenario C *Possible Answers*
5. You need to provide information regarding the number of passengers in the automobile during the accident. You also need to indicate whether any of the people in the automobile reported any injuries. You must enter the correct account number in the form.

6. You should contact J. Maldonado to obtain the missing information.

Scenario D *Possible Answers*
7. The storage cooler was locked when the delivery truck came to the store.

8. a) You can call the delivery service and request that the items be delivered later that morning. However, you may be charged for an additional delivery. b) You can leave the shelves empty until tomorrow's delivery, but your customers may be upset that they cannot purchase dairy products.

Lesson 4 (pp. 24–29)

Skill Examples
1. D   2. F   3. B   4. J

Think About It
Answers should focus on Ronaldo's and Monique's customer service skills. Ronaldo made an effort to learn about what his customer needed so he could recommend the best product. Monique did not make an effort to help her customer, so the customer spent extra time searching for the right product. Monique

could have escorted her customer to the back wall to show her specific jeans that she might like. Based on these interactions, Ronaldo seemed more knowledgeable about his store's products. Monique did not appear very knowledgeable because she did not offer her customer specific information about the different types of jeans available.

Try It Out!
1. C   2. H

Reflect
Answers should focus on whether Regina and Louis made the correct decisions in their situations and identify the effects of their decisions. Regina's customer was likely pleased that she was able to accommodate the special request. This shows that she made a good decision. Her flexibility could result in more business since customers know she is able to accommodate dietary restrictions. On the other hand, Louis upset his customer by not acting professionally and by not trying to help his customer identify alternative solutions. His decision could affect his business in the future due to customer complaints.

On Your Own
Scenario A *Possible Answers*
Step 3: a) You could see if the fixtures are available at a local store. b) You could explain to the client that the fixtures did not arrive on time and reschedule the installation for a time that is better for the client.

Step 4: Because the fixtures could be more expensive in a store and you would have to return the ones being delivered, you decide to explain to the client that the fixtures did not arrive on time and reschedule the installation for later in the week.

Step 5: You explain to the client that the fixtures did not arrive on time and reschedule the installation.

1. a) You could see if the fixtures are available at a local store. b) You could explain to the client that the fixtures did not arrive on time and reschedule the installation for another time.

2. Your solution should not involve staying late at the client's home, since the client made it clear that he does not want someone working in the evening.

3. a) You would need to call the local store to identify a price for the fixtures. b) You would need to explain to the client that there is a delay and identify a time to reschedule the installation.

Scenario B *Possible Answers*
4. a) You could give the customer the handheld blower that was ordered. b) You could give the customer the backpack blower without consulting him or her. c) You could contact the customer and let the customer know about the backpack blower and why you think it is a better fit.

5. a) The customer will probably be satisfied with the handheld blower he or she ordered. b) The customer may be upset that the blower he or she ordered is not what was received, or the customer may be happy that he or she has a backpack blower even though it is slightly more expensive. c) The customer will probably appreciate your attention to detail and your willingness to go out of your way to be sure he or she has accurate information. The customer may still decide to go with the handheld blower because he or she may be more familiar with using it or because it costs less to rent.

Scenario C *Possible Answers*
6. a) You could calmly reassure the passenger that the airline has a policy of rescheduling connecting flights and that you will share whatever information you have as soon as you get it. b) You could listen to the customer's concerns and if there is anything you can do to help, propose to help in that way. c) You could ask another gate agent to assist you with that passenger.

7. You decide to remain calm, give the customer all the information you can, and listen to the specific concerns to see how you can help.

8. The customer may trust you once you have cared enough to listen and help. If the customer is particularly irate that you have no more specific information or is still frustrated that you were not able to help with his specific concerns, he may just walk away and try to calm down on his own.

Scenario D *Possible Answers*
9. A guest has requested that you replace or fix the television in his room. You know that the hotel does not have extra televisions, but you are not sure if anyone can fix the television.

10. a) You could ask the guest if he would like to be placed in a different room with a working television. b) You could tell the guest that someone will move a working television from another room into his room. However, this may take some time to do.

11. a) The customer will be satisfied that you are fulfilling his request. b) The customer may be upset at having to wait but appreciate that he will have a working television.

Lesson 5 (pp. 32–37)

Skill Examples
1. A   2. H   3. C   4. G

Think About It
Answers should focus on Bill's and Maria's abilities to resolve conflict and cooperate with coworkers. If you were the coworker who overheard Bill's comment, you might feel hurt and angry that Bill did not respect your religious beliefs. You might feel uncomfortable working alongside Bill in the future. Maria considered her needs as well as those of her coworker and proposed a solution that was acceptable for both of them. Bill could have offered to take a different day off, or he could have tried to reschedule with his friends. Maria was much more successful in respecting the needs of others than Bill was. Maria's actions, unlike those of Bill, would be perceived favorably by coworkers and supervisors.

Try It Out!
1. E   2. F

Reflect
Answers should focus on the interpersonal skills Ricardo and Melissa demonstrated in attempting to resolve conflicts with others. Ricardo demonstrated insight in giving his employee an opportunity to discuss her actions and offering her the chance to improve her performance with guidance. Melissa did not show sensitivity in attempting to resolve the conflict with her caller. The caller was disappointed by the outcome of his loan application, but Melissa did not have to respond to his frustration with hostility. Also, her personal comments about his financial situation were both rude and unnecessary.

On Your Own
Scenario A *Possible Answers*

Step 3: a) You could tell the new employee that someone with good computer skills would not need any additional assistance. b) You could sit down with the employee and show her the basics of the programs she will need to use.

Step 4: You sit down with the employee and show her the basics of the programs she will need to use. This will help the employee develop skills in working with the computer program more quickly. This will also help build your relationship with the employee.

Step 5: You plan to set aside some time for training any time a new employee is brought into the team.

1. You chose to sit down with the employee and show her the basics of the programs she would need to use.

2. When beginning a new relationship, it is a good idea to consider diversity and not make assumptions about another person's age, race, gender, etc. Because you did this, the employee feels comfortable and knows that she can rely on you if she is not sure how to perform a task.

Scenario B *Possible Answers*

3. Since there is so much more mail to sort than usual, your supervisor is probably concerned that the work will not get done before the end of the day.

4. a) You could offer to give your supervisor hourly updates on the progress you and the other mail sorters are making. b) You could tell your supervisor to relax and stop worrying so much.

5. You could remind your supervisor of your track record of good performance under stressful situations. You could remind your supervisor that during similarly difficult days in the past, you completed all your work before the end of the day.

Scenario C *Possible Answers*

6. You might be perceived as unavailable or unapproachable by your staff.

7. You could plan to do paperwork at a different time of day, such as after lunchtime, when the restaurant is not busy.

Scenario D *Possible Answers*

8. You need to consider the needs of many different people in order to prepare yourself for any religious, ethnic, cultural, and gender-related issues and misunderstandings that may come up when people from different backgrounds work together.

9. a) You could plan to spend time working alongside each employee separately in order to get to know him or her better. b) You could have individual meetings with each team member. c) You could learn about the diverse cultures of the team members.

Lesson 6 (pp. 38–43)

Skill Examples
1. E   2. H   3. A   4. G

Think About It
Answers should focus on Toni's and Darryl's preparations for their client meetings. Toni arrived prepared to identify and remember important information. Darryl did not. Toni's actions showed that she was attentive to her client's needs. You would likely feel confident in her ability to meet your requirements. Darryl engaged his client in good conversations about the client's needs, but he was too tired to remember details. Darryl will need to contact the client again to get those details, and this could negatively affect his relationships with his client.

Try It Out!
1. C   2. F

Reflect
Answers should focus on the steps that Carly and Kelsey took to clarify any unclear details. Carly did this by asking the veterinarian clarifying questions. Kelsey, on the other hand, did not contact someone for help when he realized he was not sure of the process for locking the interior doors. He could have avoided the problem completely by having his coworker review the directions before he left.

On Your Own
Scenario A *Possible Answers*
Step 3: a) You could ignore the instructions and pick up all the forms at once. b) You could follow the instructions and pick up the forms one by one.

Step 4: You choose to follow the instructions and pick up the forms one by one. Doing so will ensure you have completed the task as required and will also ensure patient privacy.

Step 5: You follow the instructions from your supervisor and complete each form one at a time. You make trips back and forth to the printer.

1. Following the instructions exactly is the best solution. Although the instructions were complicated and may prolong the task, following your employer's policy and protecting patients' privacy take priority.

2. You could submit the forms to your supervisor for a final check.

Scenario B *Possible Answers*
3. The customer feels that you are not giving his concerns your undivided attention, implying that he is not important.

4. a) You could direct him to another employee who has more time to devote to his needs. b) You could stop trying to multitask and give the customer your undivided attention, completing your other tasks only after you have solved his problem.

Scenario C *Possible Answers*
5. Your decision does not allow you to let the focus group members offer valuable feedback on your company's new product.

6. a) You could respond to the concerns of the other members of the focus group and begin to pay more attention to their feedback. b) You could explain to the other members of the focus group that you are only looking for feedback from people who are likely to buy the product.

Scenario D *Possible Answers*
7. The store may not be prepared for the book-signing event, which could upset the customers, guests, and author.

8. a) You could have retrieved a notepad and asked your supervisor to repeat your assignments. b) You could have asked clarifying questions and confirmed orally that you knew what tasks needed to be done.

Lesson 7 (pp. 44–49)

Skill Examples
1. A   2. G   3. D   4. G

Think About It
Answers should focus on Leila's and Omar's verbal and nonverbal communication. Omar's nonverbal cues showed that he was open and welcoming to customers and confident in the products he was selling. Leila's cues showed that she was nervous, which could make her seem less confident in the products she was selling. Omar offered information about his products, such as the type of cookies available and how the products are priced. This let customers know that they had many options when choosing what to buy and that they could buy however many items they liked (since the price was by the pound). On the other hand, Leila did not provide this type of detailed information. Omar was much more successful than Leila in applying good verbal and nonverbal communication skills.

Try It Out!
1. E   2. F

Reflect
Answers should focus on preparing presentations with audiences in mind. Before creating their respective presentations, Devon and Seung needed to consider what their audiences needed or wanted to know and to consider the best way to communicate that information. The student should recognize that Devon's presentation was more successful than Seung's because she thought ahead about how she could tailor the information to best engage the children. By considering her audience ahead of time, Devon's presentation was both easy to understand and relevant for her audience. Meanwhile, Seung's presentation included details, but not the ones his supervisor asked for, making the presentation ineffective in addressing his boss's needs. By not fully considering his audience, Seung was not able to fulfill his boss's needs, resulting in wasted time and resources.

On Your Own

Scenario A *Possible Answers*

Step 3: a) You could present the information to the afternoon group the same way. b) You could reorganize your presentation based on the order the steps need to occur.

Step 4: You choose to identify the order in which the steps of enrollment need to occur and organize your presentation logically based on this order. This will help the afternoon audience understand exactly how to enroll for benefits.

Step 5: You deliver the modified presentation to the afternoon group. When you ask if there are questions, no one speaks up. One of the audience members says that the enrollment process is clear.

1. You presented the steps out of order, which confused the morning group.

2. You should reorganize the presentation so that the steps are in the correct order.

Scenario B *Possible Answers*

3. The employee's nonverbal cues tell customers that he is not interested in them and drives them away.

4. He can greet the customers when they come into the store and maintain eye contact and pay attention when they talk to him. This will meet their needs and increase business.

Scenario C *Possible Answers*

5. Your arguments were vague. They focused on routine tasks that are expected of every employee.

6. You could have focused on specific tasks that went above and beyond your regular duties and provided detailed information and statistics to demonstrate your value.

Scenario D *Possible Answers*

7. You used a lot of slang in your message. This is likely to be confusing to anyone who is not familiar with terms, such as *busted, hang tight,* and *two shakes*.

8. You could phrase your message in plain English and explain clearly that there is a broken train ahead on the track that will cause a brief delay but will be fixed soon.

Lesson 8 (pp. 50–55)

Skill Examples

1. B 2. J 3. B 4. H

Think About It

Answers should focus on the actions of Benjamin's and Gary's supervisors. Gary's supervisor took her employees' personal time into consideration. She allowed the team to work together to come to a solution that would meet the needs of the store and the employees without burdening each employee too much. Her approach was more effective in terms of working cooperatively and meeting company goals. The approach of Benjamin's supervisor was not as effective. She did not take her employees' needs into consideration and did not try to foster a sense of cooperation and teamwork. When the group does not identify with the team and its goals, the goals may not be met. In this case, the store may not have the additional coverage it needs during the sale.

Try It Out!

1. C 2. F

Reflect

Answers should focus on the process each group used. Students should recognize that Gerard's group came to a decision fairly, even though it was not the decision Gerard wanted. Gerard then showed good teamwork by accepting the team's decision despite his disappointment. Aisha made a decision based on the majority view, claiming it was what everyone wanted. The group had not, in fact, reached an agreement, and those holding the minority view were particularly upset. Aisha can now try to rebuild teamwork by acknowledging the importance of making decisions as a group and by promising to work toward compromise in the future.

On Your Own

Scenario A *Possible Answers*

Step 3: a) You could confront Heather about her bad attitude in the classroom. b) You could explain to Heather that her suggestions were interesting but not practical.

Step 4: You explain to Heather that her suggestions were interesting but not practical. You choose this solution because it allows you to explain your choices clearly, while helping her feel like a valued and creative member of the team.

Step 5: You explain to Heather why her suggestions are interesting but not practical. You thank her for her enthusiasm and offer to implement some of her other ideas that are more practical in the classroom.

1. You can thank her for her innovative approach to the classroom design and include her in future projects where her unique viewpoint will be valuable.

2. If Heather feels valued, she may be more enthusiastic when working with the children and more eager to help you. She may also contribute more ideas that could be helpful. If she does not feel valued, she may be less likely to help out or offer ideas that may benefit you or the class.

Scenario B *Possible Answers*

3. Your crew underestimates the amount of work you do and does not feel that you are dividing up the work fairly.

4. a) You could take on more of the physically demanding jobs and work additional hours to complete your paperwork. b) You could explain in detail the tasks you must do before crew members arrive and after they leave.

5. a) You might have to work overtime to finish all of your work. b) Your crew might have a greater understanding of why you are not able to help out with the physically demanding tasks.

Scenario C *Possible Answers*

6. Your team is not sure what you are asking for with regards to the commercial. You have not explained the purpose of the meeting or the value of developing a commercial.

7. You can give the team members detailed assignments for them to work on before the next meeting, such as asking them to think of two fun slogans and one design idea.

Scenario D *Possible Answers*

8. Your sales force tends to submit reports late. This causes a conflict with your supervisor, who does not understand the time constraints you are under when you have to complete your reports.

9. You can explain to the supervisor that the problem is caused by the salespeople's lateness in getting you reports and ask him or her to require them to submit their reports in a more timely manner.

Lesson 9 (pp. 58–63)

Skill Examples
1. C   2. F   3. A   4. G

Think About It
Answers should focus on Daniela's and Mark's behavior toward their coworkers. Daniela prioritized her tasks according to her personal feelings about her coworkers rather than according to the importance of the task. Her behavior was biased and unethical. Mark was better able to balance his personal feelings with his work responsibilities. He was willing to report his coworker's poor hygiene even though it meant risking a friendship. His actions demonstrate integrity.

Try It Out!
1. D   2. K

Reflect
Answers should focus on the factors that Juanita and Caleb took into consideration when making their decisions and how these factors resulted in both of

them making the correct choices. Juanita realized that she had to make a decision based on what was best for her company rather than what was best for herself. Caleb put himself in the customer's position, realized how he would feel if he lost $20, and encouraged his coworker to return the money. Had Juanita and Caleb acted in a less ethical manner and been discovered, they might have been reprimanded or even fired.

On Your Own
Scenario A *Possible Answers*
Step 3: a) You could admit your mistake. b) You could allow the junior stagehand to take the blame.

Step 4: You choose to admit your mistake and let the master carpenter know that it was not the junior stagehand's fault. You do this because admitting your mistake is the honest thing to do.

Step 5: You have a quiet word with the master carpenter, apologize for the error, and tell him you will rebuild the table so that it is the correct shape.

1. a) You could admit the mistake. b) You could allow the junior stagehand to take the blame.

2. a) If you admit the mistake, you could risk your reputation as a competent worker but earn the respect of your coworkers for behaving ethically. b) If you allow the junior stagehand to take the blame, you would escape disciplinary action but risk earning a reputation as an unethical employee.

Scenario B *Possible Answers*
3. You are being asked to share privileged information about your previous company.

4. You tell your supervisor that you are unwilling to share privileged information about your former employer's clients.

5. You might speak with your supervisor. If your supervisor does not respond to your initial statement that you will not share information, ask to speak with your supervisor's boss.

Scenario C *Possible Answers*
6. a) You could try to get your friends' child into the after-school program. b) You could explain to your friends that it would be unethical to use your position to get their child into the program. c) You could use your knowledge as a childcare development specialist to provide your friends with a list of alternative after-school programs.

7. a) You might be reprimanded for your actions, but your friends would be grateful. b) You might risk your friendship, but you would keep your reputation as a fair and ethical employee. c) You would demonstrate a willingness to help your friends while maintaining your professional reputation.

Scenario D *Possible Answers*

8. Your team erected the scaffolding earlier than scheduled. You are expected to check in for more tasks when you complete the assigned task. Your staff wants to leave without checking in.

9. Call your boss and explain that your team has erected the scaffolding earlier than anticipated. Give your boss the option of assigning you another task or allowing you to leave early.

Lesson 10 (pp. 64–69)

Skill Examples
1. A   2. G   3. C   4. G

Think About It
Answers should focus on Mei's and Gunther's willingness to take responsibility for their actions and the possible consequences of their actions. In *Example 1*, Mei did not take responsibility for her actions because she refused to admit that she had made a mistake and argued back to the customer. Her behavior could get her fired and cause negative word of mouth about the deli. In *Example 2*, Gunther took responsibility for his mistake by apologizing, offering to correct the problem as soon as possible, and returning to the customer's house early the next day to fix it. Even though Gunther quickly corrected the problem, he may receive a verbal reprimand from his supervisor for not checking the wiring before leaving the customer's home. Because Gunther reacted quickly, this is less likely to have a negative effect on the company. If Gunther had refused to admit his mistake to the customer or return to the house to fix the problem, his relationship with the customer would be severely damaged. The customer would lose confidence in him and possibly in the company.

Try It Out!
1. A   2. J

Reflect
Answers should focus on the likely outcome of Sunil's and Miles's actions. Sunil made the right decision because he took responsibility for his actions and did not try to cover up his mistake. Had he not told his boss about the missing ten minutes of the recording, he might have created future problems for his company. Miles also made the correct decision because he showed his boss that he was willing to take on responsibilities outside of his job description. Had Miles refused to help in the accounting department, the boss might have concluded that Miles was inflexible and unwilling to work as part of a team.

On Your Own
Scenario A *Possible Answers*

Step 3: a) You could return to check on the customer. b) You could assume the customer has already left.

Step 4: You choose to return to check on the customer. Since it is possible that she is still waiting, you should not assume that she has left. Checking on the customer provides the best customer service.

Step 5: You explain the situation, apologize to the customer, and make assisting her a top priority.

1. a) You could check on the customer. b) You could assume the customer has already left.

2. You chose to return to the dressing room and check on the customer. In the future, you might refer customers to another sales assistant if you are already busy helping someone else.

Scenario B *Possible Answers*

3. You choose to try to clean the suits using a different stain-removing product. To avoid the same mistake, you test a spot of the product where a mark would not be noticed.

4. By spot testing a different cleaning solution, you may take longer to clean the suit. However, by taking this step, you will know whether or not the solution will remove the stain without damaging the suit.

Scenario C *Possible Answers*

5. a) You could hope that the client does not notice that the bush is different. b) You could return to the customer's house and replace the bush again without consulting the customer. c) You could explain the situation to the client.

6. You choose to explain the situation to the client and offer to replace the bush as soon as possible. This is the responsible solution because the client asked for your help in maintaining her plant. It is also the best solution because if you do not correct the mistake, the client may make negative comments about your business to other people. This solution is better than option b, since changing the bush without consulting your client could create confusion and further undermine the client's trust in you.

Scenario D *Possible Answers*

7. a) You could volunteer for the event, which would demonstrate to your supervisor that you are willing to work but require that you change your weekend plans. b) You could keep quiet, which might give your supervisor the impression that you are unwilling to help but enable you to keep your weekend plans.

8. You choose to volunteer for the extra shift. Volunteering shows your supervisor that you are flexible and willing to work extra hours. You figure that you can always make plans for a future free weekend.

Lesson 11 (pp. 70–75)

Skill Examples
1. E   2. H   3. C   4. H

Think About It
Answers should focus on Marisol's and Golda's ability to prioritize. In *Example 1*, Marisol did not prioritize her tasks. Instead, she tried to complete her assigned task of archiving magazines while also working on her standard tasks at the same time. Marisol could have changed the outcome of the day by prioritizing and completing the cataloging first. In the future, when Marisol knows she will have a busy day, she can think about what tasks will need to be her top priority. Also, Marisol can ask her supervisor for help with some of the tasks or let her supervisor know that some of her regular tasks will have to be completed on another day. In *Example 2*, Golda looked at her upcoming schedule and was able to plan a way to prioritize her tasks. She made sure to complete another assignment before leaving for the day and arrived at the lab early the next day so she would have time to finish testing all of the samples.

Try It Out!
1. A   2. H

Reflect
Answers should focus on the information that Jacques and Sanibel had available to them and whether they used the information to reach the correct decision. Jacques knew that a large conference would be coming to town the following month and he would need additional staff. He used this information to determine that he needed to revise his schedule. Sanibel knew that her client had a problem with the SQL server. She also knew that certain materials would be needed to complete the task. However, she did not use this information to prepare herself adequately. She should have made sure that she had everything she was likely to need before she left the office.

On Your Own
Scenario A *Possible Answers*

Step 3: a) You could hire extra farmhands. b) You could try to manage the additional work yourself.

Step 4: You choose to hire extra farmhands to free up your time for administrative and managerial tasks.

Step 5: You research the best way to hire reliable and experienced employees.

1. a) You could hire extra farmhands. b) You could try to manage the additional work yourself.

2. a) You choose to hire extra farmhands. The advantages to this solution are that it allows you to spend more time on the administrative and managerial tasks. The disadvantages are that it takes time and effort to find good employees and costs the farm additional time and resources. b) You choose to manage the additional work yourself. The advantages to this solution are that you do not need to hire and train new staff members. The disadvantage is that you may not be able to keep up with the work yourself.

Scenario B *Possible Answers*

3. You are not sure if you should focus on cleaning the rooms on the hotel's priority list or continue cleaning rooms from the bottom up.

4. a) You could continue to use your system. The pro for this is that you can clearly identify which rooms have been cleaned and which still need to be cleaned. The con is that some hotel guests may not be able to check in because their rooms are not ready. b) You could begin focusing on the rooms identified in the hotel's priority list. The pro for this solution is that when hotel guests arrive to check in, their rooms will be ready for them. The con is that you will have to go from floor to floor, which may be less effective than completing one floor at a time.

5. Stopping what you are doing and following the hotel's prioritizing system would demonstrate that you are able to prioritize. Following this system would ensure that the guests' rooms are cleaned on time. It would also show that you are following your employer's system.

Scenario C *Possible Answers*

6. You choose to tell your current customer that you have another appointment but will return at the end of the day to complete her job.

7. You would need to let the first customer know that you must leave to attend to another client but will be back later that day to complete the job.

Scenario D *Possible Answers*

8. a) You could transfer the colored ink to the store with the large order. b) You could transfer the order to the store with the needed ink.

9. You choose to transfer the ink to the store with the large order. You think this decision is more convenient for the customer. By transferring the ink, the customer can pick up the order from the store where he or she placed the order.

Lesson 12 (pp. 76–81)

Skill Examples

1. C   2. F   3. B   4. F

Think About It

Answers should focus on Renata's and Herschel's attitudes, behaviors, and impressions. Renata allowed a bad experience with a customer to affect her treatment of other patrons in the restaurant. This behavior may cause others to think that she is unprofessional. Herschel maintained his temper and spoke to his coworker calmly and politely. Because Herschel treated his coworker respectfully, he is more likely to not only receive the same treatment in return but also to be perceived as a respectful person. Thus, Herschel is more likely to retain the respect of his coworkers. If Renata were to change her behavior and act more professionally, she might regain the respect of her coworkers and help secure her job. If Herschel were to change his behavior and start yelling at Lou, he might damage his relationship with Lou. He might also lose the respect of his coworkers.

Try It Out!

1. B   2. F

Reflect

Answers should focus on Rosette's and Miguel's decisions. Rosette made the right decision because she chose to speak with her manager about how her work was affecting her home life. Had she chosen an alternative option, she might have risked her family's happiness or developed a stress-related illness. Miguel also made the right decision because he kept his temper and spoke to the customer firmly but politely. He referred the customer to the manager, the person who has the power to meet her demands. Had he lost his temper, Miguel might have lost his job and the customer's business.

On Your Own

Scenario A *Possible Answers*

Step 3: a) You could use your lunch break to return home and change. b) You could remain in the office in your casual clothes.

Step 4: You choose to go home at lunch and change. You want to make a good impression for the client and also follow the company's policy. Your lunch break is a good time to leave the office to change.

Step 5: You leave enough time to return home, change, and make it back to the office before the client arrives.

1. a) You could use your lunch break to return home and change. b) You could remain in the office in your casual clothes.

2. Whichever option you choose, you should inform your supervisor, because you will either be absent from the office for a period of time or potentially showing the company in a bad light. You should arrange a personal meeting with your supervisor to discuss the situation.

Scenario B *Possible Answers*

3. You have to focus on your work, but you are being distracted by a personal problem.

4. a) You could ignore your friend's calls and e-mails until after work. b) You could spend your workday replying to your friend's e-mails to resolve the argument. c) You could make one phone call to your friend to let him or her know that you cannot discuss the matter at work. You will call your friend as soon as you arrive home.

5. Ignoring your friend's calls and e-mails during work hours would best demonstrate professionalism. Making one phone call to your friend would also demonstrate professionalism, as long as you return to your assignments as soon as the conversation ends.

Scenario C *Possible Answers*

6. You have to implement an idea that you do not like.

7. a) You could ignore your manager and create your preferred holiday display. b) You could put on a positive face and create the manager's chosen holiday display.

8. Putting on a positive face and creating the manager's chosen display would demonstrate that you are a professional employee.

Scenario D *Possible Answers*

9. a) You could ask your manager for a spare shirt. b) You could skip classes occasionally to do your laundry.

10. Asking your manager for a spare shirt would best demonstrate that you are an employee with a healthy work-life balance. The other option indicates that you do not have a healthy work-life balance.

Skill Examples

1. E   2. G   3. D   4. J

Think About It

Answers should focus on the efforts Jackson and Lavina put in to complete their tasks. Jackson did not take the initiative to plan his assigned tasks, nor did he communicate with anyone about his workload being unmanageable. This lack of forethought led to his not calling the client in time. Lavina, in contrast, planned both her personal and professional commitments carefully and was able to accomplish her task by working overtime. Although this solution was effective, both Lavina and Jackson need to be proactive and take initiative by talking to their supervisors if their workload continues to be excessive.

Try It Out!

1. C   2. F

Reflect

Answers should focus on whether Roger and Amina showed good judgment in how they chose to handle a problem. Roger showed good judgment while working independently because he chose a company-approved resource. Had he used outside resources, he might have found inaccurate information. Amina showed poor judgment. Making a demand and threatening to quit are never good strategies to use when trying to advance at work. Instead, Amina should have approached her manager with a plan for how she could accomplish her goal. Had she done so, she would have had a chance to learn without putting her reputation and employment at risk.

On Your Own

Scenario A *Possible Answers*

Step 3: a) You could talk to other stylists about local cosmetology programs. b) You could look up information about local cosmetology programs online. c) You could tell other coworkers or your supervisor about your goal and ask what information they could provide.

Step 4: You choose to tell other coworkers or your supervisor about your goal and ask what information they could provide. This choice allows you to consult a variety of familiar and credible sources.

Step 5: You discuss your goal with your supervisor and ask for suggestions on how you can go about achieving it.

1. a) You could talk to other stylists about local cosmetology programs. b) You could look up information about local cosmetology programs online. c) You could tell other coworkers or your supervisor about your goal and ask what information they could provide.

2. Choosing to speak with your supervisor would show that you are working to achieve your goals. You can also discuss your long-term plans with your boss and enquire about receiving financial assistance and training from your employer.

Scenario B *Possible Answers*

3. You need to decide how to proceed since you cannot complete the task you planned.

4. a) You could stop work until the shipment arrives, but this will delay completion of the project. b) You could work on the weight room. c) You could try to find the supplies in another place, such as a local hardware store.

5. Working on the weight room would allow you to continue your work despite the obstacle presented by the delayed shipment. Waiting for the delayed shipment could cause you to run behind schedule.

Scenario C *Possible Answers*

6. a) You could take care of the other tasks that need to be completed. b) You could let your supervisor know that you completed the assigned task early and ask her what you should work on next.

7. Informing your supervisor that you have completed the assigned task and that you are now working on completing other routine tasks would ensure that your day is as productive as possible.

8. You should inform your supervisor that you finished the task early and explain how this was possible. Communicating this information lets your supervisor know that you did not rush through the task. It also gives you a chance to contribute to the company's overall productivity, since you will have shown your supervisor a more efficient way to do a routine task. You should also let your supervisor know what you are working on next.

Scenario D *Possible Answers*

9. One way to solve the problem would be to stay at school until 5:00 P.M. once or twice a week. You could also tutor the student before school or on the weekend.

10. By giving up your personal time to accommodate the student, you would show that you are really interested in helping the student succeed. It also would show that you love and enjoy the work you do and are willing to make some sacrifices to do your job well.

Lesson 14 (pp. 90–95)

Skill Examples

1. C   2. H   3. D   4. K

Think About It

Answers should focus on Cesar's and Chang's willingness to tolerate ambiguity and generate alternative solutions. Cesar refused to consider any explanation other than his original idea—even when the customer suggested there might be another problem. Chang took time to gather data about the problem and explore multiple causes. As a result, Chang was able to solve the problem, while Cesar was not. Cesar also risked offending the customer. Chang's approach to problems was effective and does not need to be changed. Cesar needs to learn how to consider multiple causes and solutions.

Try It Out!

1. D   2. G

Reflect

Answers should focus on the consequences of Sarita's and Maor's actions. Sarita's approach was effective because she pinpointed the cause of the problem and suggested a way to improve the payroll process. Her suggestion has the potential to improve company efficiency. Maor's approach was not effective. It did nothing to reduce his team's call volume, improve customer service, or improve productivity. Instead, Maor should have spoken to his supervisor about including routine shipping information on the company website. He should have explained that doing so would help his team focus on more important customer issues and, therefore, allow the company to provide excellent customer service.

On Your Own

Scenario A *Possible Answers*

Step 3: a) You could choose not to serve refreshments. b) You could estimate the amount of refreshments needed and order that much. c) You could ask the speaker's event-planning team how many people registered.

Step 4: You choose to ask the speaker's event-planning team how many people registered. This will give you the information you need to prepare.

Step 5: You contact the speaker's event-planning team and ask them how many people have registered.

1. a) You could choose not to serve refreshments. b) You could estimate the amount of refreshments needed and order that much. c) You could ask the speaker's event-planning team how many people registered for the event.

2. You need to communicate with the event-planning team. This will help you purchase just

the right amount of refreshments. Eliminating refreshments would reflect poorly on the hotel and you. Estimating the amount of refreshments needed could result in too much or too little food.

Scenario B *Possible Answers*

3. Sometimes files are misplaced, and you cannot find them. You and your manager think the filing system is inefficient. Your manager says the office cannot afford an electronic system.

4. a) You could suggest the electronic filing system to another manager. b) You could ask for assistance with filing tasks. c) You could research more affordable electronic filing systems. You choose the third option since you think that cost would be an issue with the other options.

5. Researching cheaper electronic filing options would show that you can be creative when additional resources, such as expensive technology, are not affordable.

Scenario C *Possible Answers*

6. The problem is that you want to use social media for marketing but do not know how to use it to reach your target audience.

7. a) You could ask your niece how she uses social media. b) You could contact the marketing company for information.

8. As a starting point of your research, you choose to ask your niece about marketing through social media. At seventeen, she is familiar with your target audience, high school students. She probably knows how they use social media, and she has marketed products through social media.

Scenario D *Possible Answers*

9. a) You could explain the situation to your client and suggest alternative dessert choices. b) You could try to obtain lemons from another source, such as a different wholesaler or a local supermarket. a) By suggesting alternative dessert choices, you might upset your client who has specifically asked for lemon meringue pie. b) By trying to obtain lemons from another source, you can impress your client with your resourcefulness.

10. a) If you are considering an alternative dessert, you will need to discuss possibilities with your client and staff. b) If you decide to obtain lemons from another source, you will need to communicate with the supplier and with your staff.

Lesson 15 (pp. 96–101)

Skill Examples

1. C   2. J   3. E   4. J

Think About It

Answers should focus on how Jamal and Amar viewed the training opportunities and the decisions they made about whether or not to attend. Jamal attended a training session for the new tool and discussed what he had learned with his supervisor. Amar assumed he did not need training, and as a result, he later had difficulty using the tool. This impaired his performance and eventually necessitated that he come in on his own time to learn. Jamal's choice is likely to impress his supervisor, and if his skills improve, it benefits the company. Amar's lack of training may interfere with his ability to meet deadlines and do his work well, which could give his supervisor and customers a negative impression.

Try It Out!

1. B   2. F

Reflect

Answers should focus on the consequences of Liesel's and Sharif's actions. Liesel made the right decision because her colleague benefited from her computer skills, and she was able to help him while still completing her own work. If she had chosen not to help her colleague, he might have failed to meet his deadline, which could negatively affect the entire office. Sharif was wrong in his decision to not have his employees trained on the new registers. In addition, because he decided not to set up training, he should have anticipated that his employees would need time to become well-versed in using the new registers. It also would have been a good idea to inform customers about possible delays in the checkout process.

On Your Own

Scenario A *Possible Answers*

Step 3: a) You could try to fix the wiring based on your memory. b) You could go to the factory where you had a similar problem and see how you fixed it. c) You could review your notes on how you fixed the problem the last time and then go to repair the wiring.

Step 4: You choose to review your notes on how you first fixed the wiring and then solve the problem. This way, you know for sure how you fixed the problem and are able to do it without wasting time.

Step 5: You refer to your notes on how to fix the problem and then take the necessary steps to solve it.

1. a) You could try to fix the wiring based on your memory. b) You could review your notes on how you fixed the problem the last time, and then go to repair the wiring.

2. You review your notes on how you fixed the wiring before and then solve the problem. By referring to your notes, you know for sure how you fixed the problem and are able to do it without wasting time.

Scenario B *Possible Answers*

3. a) You could tell your supervisor that you cannot put in extra hours because of your personal commitments. By doing this, you would give a bad impression to your supervisor about your professional dedication. b) You could make plans with friends or family to have your son cared for while you put in extra hours at work. This would show your supervisor that you are willing to put in extra effort in order to do your job well.

4. You choose to make plans with friends or family to have your son cared for while you put in extra hours at work. You do this to show your supervisor that you are willing to put in the extra effort in order to do your job well.

Scenario C *Possible Answers*

5. a) You could ask another coworker to help Debra. b) You could offer to do the presentation for Debra. c) You could ask Debra to show you how to put together a few slides, and then complete the rest of the presentation for her.

6. Solution c) would show that you know how to employ learning strategies. This solution involves having a coworker guide you through an unfamiliar process before attempting it yourself.

Scenario D *Possible Answers*

7. The problem is that your newspaper is switching to a new word-processing program that is very different from the one you currently use. You are worried that you will have trouble using it.

8. a) You could try to learn the new program on your own after the paper makes the change, but this could significantly affect your productivity during the learning period. b) You could wait to see if your employer will provide training after installing the new program. If your employer does not offer training, you will not be able to learn the program in advance. c) You could sign up for a tutorial at the community college, which would ensure that you learn the program regardless of whether or not your employer provides training.

Lesson 16 (pp. 102–107)

Skill Examples

1. B   2. H   3. B   4. J

Think About It

Answers should focus on Alexander's and Lucille's situational awareness and how each responded to a situation in which they needed more information or help. Alexander needed help in completing the inventory accurately but did not ask for it. Lucille needed more information about the problem with the cameras, so she took time to check each one. As a result, she was able to gauge the extent of the problem before reporting it. Alexander's inaccurate inventory resulted in the warehouse not being stocked adequately. Lucille was aware of how her work fit within the larger company. She made sure to check all the cameras before reporting the problem to her boss. By doing so, she was able to give her boss a global picture of the problem. Alexander, however, was unaware of how his job impacted others. He did not seek help when he needed it. By doing his job poorly, he negatively affected the company.

Try It Out!

1. B   2. K

Reflect

Answers should focus on the consequences of Mel's and Chloe's actions. Mel made the right decision by gathering additional information and presenting it to his boss. Had he not done so, his boss might not have known about trends for spring and thus would not have prepared for these trends. As a result, he probably would have lost a lot of business. Chloe did not make a good decision. She should have explained to the manager that based on her experience, the restaurant would probably be very busy next week, so he should order more food. Doing so would have minimized the risk of running out of supplies and possibly losing or upsetting customers.

On Your Own

Scenario A *Possible Answers*

Step 3: a) You could stay and finish the job. b) You could go home early. c) You could explain the situation to the team and then together decide how to proceed.

Step 4: You choose to explain the situation to the team and work together to decide how to proceed. This allows you to gather more information to help you make a sound decision.

Step 5: You talk with the team about the situation and then together decide how to proceed.

1. You explain the situation to the team and then together decide how to proceed.

2. You would need to communicate with the team (and perhaps your supervisor) about how the work schedule would be affected and how tasks should be rescheduled.

Scenario B *Possible Answers*

3. a) You could go to the restaurant, but you may be bored there. b) You could go to the dance club, but doing so might tarnish your image.

4. The most appropriate choice is to have dinner with senior management. Because the club has a questionable reputation, it is not wise to go there while traveling for business. Also, customers are in the area and may be at the same places you are planning on going. Since you are representing your company, your behavior during this trip must be professional, even during off hours.

Scenario C *Possible Answers*

5. The problem is that your client wants you to take a certain approach to designing the logo, but based on your research, you would like to take a different approach.

6. a) You could disregard your research and follow the client's suggested approach. b) You could ignore the customer's instruction and create the logo the way you want. c) You could discuss your concerns with the client and try to find a design approach you can both agree upon.

7. The most effective way to meet your client's needs would be to share your professional expertise and then try to work out an approach you can both agree upon. Communicating with the client would demonstrate that you care about making the best choice for his business.

Scenario D *Possible Answers*

8. Your close friend is your materials supplier. Her profits will increase or decrease depending on the materials your client chooses. Your client can afford expensive materials; however, she has simple tastes and might be satisfied with less expensive materials.

9. a) You could present your client with only the most expensive materials, but this would not be fair to her, because it would not give her a complete understanding of her options. b) You could present your client with options from all price ranges and let her make a decision. Doing so would be the most honest course of action and could strengthen your business's reputation.